Affirmations Moms Actually Need

Nurturing Your Mind, Heart, and Spirit on the Journey of Motherhood

Michelle Mann

Contents

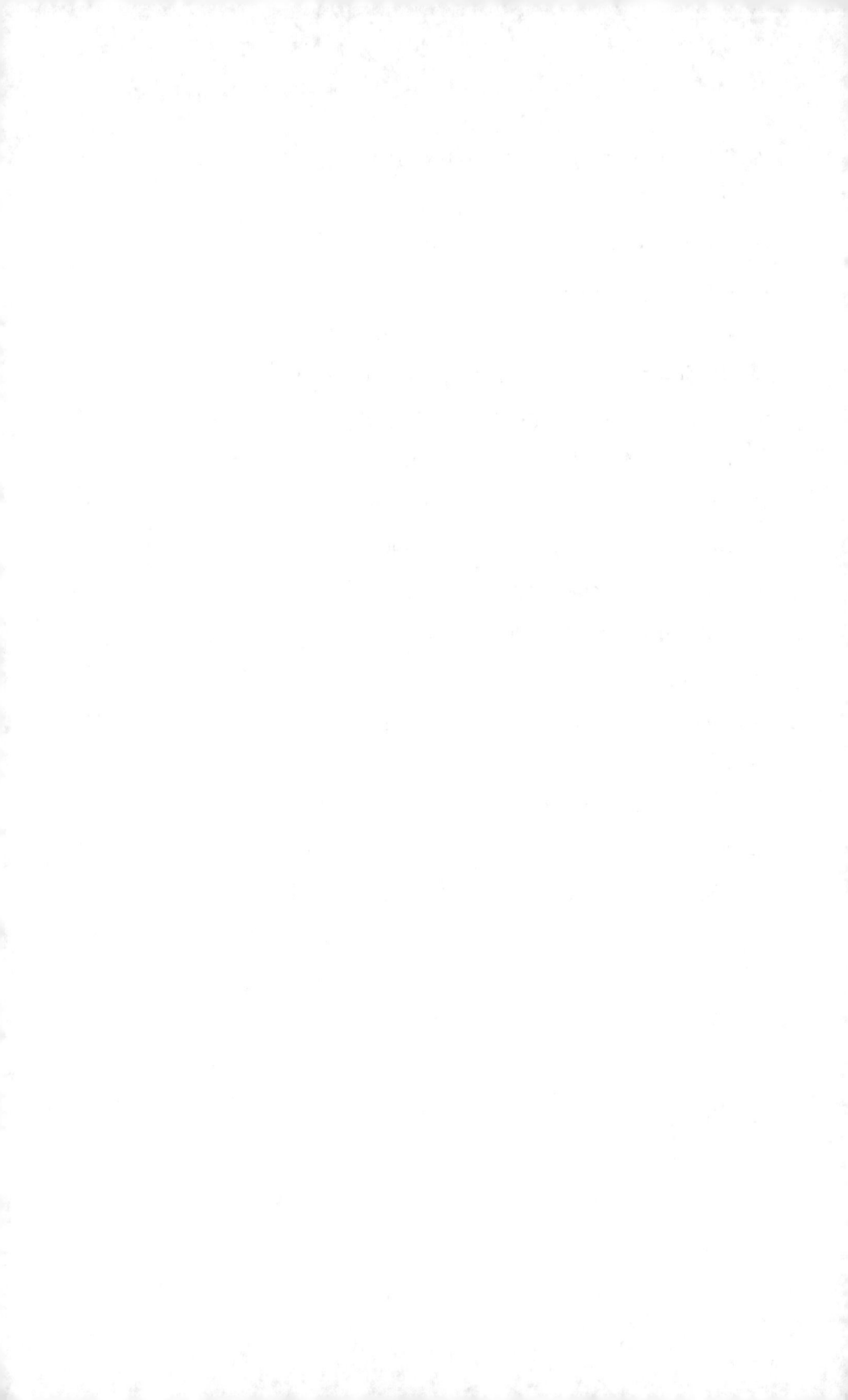

Introduction

B eing a mom is a beautiful and rewarding experience, but it also comes with its fair share of challenges and demands. From the moment you hold your child in your arms, your life transforms in ways you never imagined. Amidst the joy and love, there are moments of self-doubt, exhaustion, and overwhelming responsibilities.

In the midst of all the chaos and busyness, it's essential for moms to prioritize their own well-being and nurture their mental and emotional health. This is where the power of affirmations comes in. Affirmations are positive statements that can shift your mindset, boost your confidence, and help you navigate the rollercoaster of motherhood with greater resilience and self-compassion.

"Affirmations Moms Actually Need" is a book designed specifically for moms, providing a collection of empowering and uplifting affirmations tailored to address the unique needs and struggles they face. This book is not just another self-help guide; it's a loving companion that will remind you of your strength, worthiness, and the incredible job you're doing as a mom.

In this book, you will embark on a journey of self-discovery, self-care, and self-empowerment. Each chapter is carefully crafted to offer guidance, support, and practical tools to help you cultivate a positive mindset, overcome self-doubt, and embrace the joys and challenges of motherhood.

Through the pages of "Affirmations Moms Actually Need," you will discover the power of self-care and how it nourishes your soul. You'll learn to release the burden of mom guilt and embrace imperfections with love and acceptance. Building resilience will become second nature as you face the inevitable ups and downs of life.

Nurturing your relationships will be emphasized, as you strengthen connections with your partner, friends, and most importantly, with your children. By harnessing the power of positive self-talk and practicing gratitude, you'll elevate your confidence and find beauty in the ordinary moments of motherhood. Mindfulness will become a daily practice, allowing you to savor the present and find calm amidst the chaos.

This book is not about striving for perfection or pretending that motherhood is always easy. It's about honoring the journey, embracing your authentic self, and recognizing that you are enough. As you delve into the affirmations and concepts presented here, you will find that you are not alone in your experiences. You are part of a community of moms who are navigating similar paths and who are also seeking love, understanding, and support.

So, dear mom, take a deep breath, open your heart, and allow the affirmations in this book to remind you of your inner strength and the incredible impact you have on the lives of your children. May these affirmations serve as a gentle reminder that you are worthy, deserving, and capable of embracing the fullness of motherhood while nurturing your own well-being.

Are you ready to embark on this transformative journey? Let's dive in and discover the affirmations moms actually need.

Importance of affirmations for moms

A s a mom, your role is multifaceted and demanding. From managing household responsibilities to nurturing your children's growth and development, your days are filled with constant action and selflessness. In the midst of this whirlwind, it's easy to neglect your own needs and lose sight of your intrinsic value as an individual.

Affirmations play a crucial role in supporting your well-being as a mom. They are powerful tools that can positively influence your thoughts, emotions, and actions. By intentionally choosing and repeating affirmations, you can reshape your mindset, boost your self-esteem, and cultivate a more positive and empowering inner dialogue.

1. Nurturing self-belief: Motherhood often brings forth self-doubt and feelings of inadequacy. Affirmations provide a counterbalance to these negative thoughts, reinforcing your belief in your abilities as a mom. They remind you that you are doing your best, that you are capable of handling challenges, and that you are deserving of love and respect.

2. Building resilience: Motherhood can be a rollercoaster ride, filled with unexpected twists and turns. Affirmations act as anchors during difficult times, helping you build resilience and navigate the storms with greater strength and determination. They remind you of your inherent strength and inspire you to persevere when faced with setbacks or overwhelming moments.

3. Cultivating self-care: As a mom, it's essential to prioritize self-care to maintain your physical, mental, and emotional well-being. Affirmations can serve as gentle reminders to carve out time for yourself, set boundaries, and engage in activities that bring you joy and rejuvenation. They encourage you to embrace self-care practices without guilt, understanding that taking care of yourself ultimately benefits both you and your family.

4. Shifting mindset and perspective: Affirmations have the power to transform negative thought patterns into positive ones. They challenge limiting beliefs and help you reframe challenges as opportunities for growth. By consciously choosing affirmations that promote optimism, gratitude, and self-compassion, you can shift your mindset and cultivate a more positive outlook on motherhood and life.

5. Enhancing emotional well-being: Motherhood is an emotional journey, and it's important to nurture your emotional well-being along the way. Affirmations can support you in managing stress, reducing anxiety, and promoting a sense of inner calm. They provide a source of comfort, reassurance, and stability during moments of emotional turbulence.

By incorporating affirmations into your daily routine, you create space for self-reflection, self-empowerment, and self-acceptance. They become a source of strength and encouragement, reminding you of your worthiness, resilience, and the profound impact you have as a mom.

In the pages of this book, you will discover a treasure trove of affirmations specifically curated to address the unique needs and challenges faced by moms. These affirmations will serve as gentle whispers of support, reminding you of your inherent strength, beauty, and the incredible journey you are undertaking as a mom.

How affirmations can positively impact mental and emotional well-being

Motherhood is a beautiful and fulfilling journey, but it can also be emotionally challenging. The constant demands, sleepless nights, and overwhelming responsibilities can take a toll on your mental and emotional well-being. Affirmations offer a powerful tool to support and uplift your mental and emotional state, fostering resilience, positivity, and self-compassion.

1. Shifting negative self-talk: Affirmations combat the negative self-talk that often plagues moms. They challenge and replace self-limiting beliefs with positive and empowering statements. By repeating affirmations that counteract negative thoughts, you can gradually shift your internal dialogue and cultivate a more compassionate and supportive mindset.

2. Boosting self-esteem: Motherhood can sometimes make you question your worth and abilities. Affirmations serve as reminders of your inherent value and strengths as a mom. By consistently affirming your skills, qualities, and accomplishments, you can boost your self-esteem and develop a more confident and positive self-perception.

3. Fostering resilience: Affirmations play a vital role in building emotional re-

silience. They help you develop a mindset that embraces challenges as opportunities for growth and learning. By repeating affirmations that encourage perseverance, adaptability, and inner strength, you can navigate the ups and downs of motherhood with greater resilience and bounce back from setbacks more easily.

4. Cultivating gratitude and positivity: Affirmations can shift your focus towards gratitude and positivity, even in challenging times. By choosing affirmations that promote appreciation, joy, and optimism, you can reframe your perspective and cultivate a mindset of abundance and contentment. This shift in mindset can enhance your overall mental and emotional well-being.

5. Managing stress and anxiety: Motherhood can bring about stress and anxiety. Affirmations can be powerful tools for managing these emotions. By repeating affirmations that promote calmness, peace, and self-soothing, you can create a sense of inner balance and reduce stress levels. Affirmations also serve as gentle reminders to take care of yourself and prioritize self-care, which is crucial for managing and alleviating stress.

6. Nurturing self-compassion: Affirmations encourage self-compassion, reminding you to be kind to yourself and embrace self-care. They help you cultivate a nurturing and understanding attitude towards yourself, acknowledging that it's okay to make mistakes and that self-love is a fundamental part of your well-being. By practicing self-compassionate affirmations, you can foster a healthier and more resilient relationship with yourself.

Incorporating affirmations into your daily routine allows you to intentionally focus on positive thoughts and emotions. They serve as gentle reminders to prioritize self-care, embrace self-acceptance, and cultivate a positive mindset. As you consistently practice affirmations, you will notice a transformation in your mental and emotional well-being, experiencing increased resilience, self-esteem, and overall happiness.

In the upcoming chapters of this book, you will discover a wide range of affirmations specifically designed to support your mental and emotional well-being as a mom. These affirmations will empower you, nurture your inner self, and help you navigate the beautiful and challenging aspects of motherhood with grace and positivity.

Brief explanation of the book's purpose and content

"**A**ffirmations Moms Actually Need" is a book created with the purpose of providing moms with a valuable resource to support their mental, emotional, and spiritual well-being. It is a comprehensive guide that offers a collection of affirmations tailored specifically to address the unique challenges, joys, and self-care needs of mothers.

The content of this book is divided into several chapters, each focusing on a specific aspect of a mom's journey. From embracing self-care to overcoming mom guilt, building resilience, and nurturing relationships, each chapter delves deep into essential areas of a mother's life.

The book begins with an introduction that highlights the importance of affirmations for moms, explaining how they can positively impact mental and emotional well-being. It emphasizes the significance of self-belief, resilience, self-care, and mindset shifts to navigate the joys and challenges of motherhood.

Throughout the chapters, you will find a rich collection of affirmations accompanied by insights, reflections, and practical tips. The affirmations are carefully crafted to resonate with the experiences and emotions that mothers commonly encounter. They serve as powerful reminders to help you cultivate self-compassion, embrace imperfections, and prioritize your well-being amidst the busyness of motherhood.

The book covers various topics essential for moms, including:

1. Embracing Self-Care: This chapter explores the significance of self-care for

moms and offers affirmations to support you in nurturing yourself and setting healthy boundaries.

2. Overcoming Mom Guilt: Here, you will find affirmations that address the common struggle of mom guilt and guide you towards self-forgiveness and self-acceptance.

3. Building Resilience: This chapter focuses on developing resilience in the face of challenges and change. Affirmations are provided to inspire inner strength and adaptability.

4. Embracing Imperfections: Celebrating imperfections and cultivating self-love are the key themes of this chapter. Affirmations encourage self-acceptance and the appreciation of the unique journey of motherhood.

5. Nurturing Relationships: Relationships are explored in this chapter, offering affirmations to enhance communication, strengthen connections, and foster meaningful relationships with partners, friends, and children.

6. Empowering Mom's Inner Voice: Affirmations in this chapter help you harness the power of positive self-talk, fostering self-belief, and confidence in your abilities as a mom.

7. Practicing Gratitude: Gratitude is explored as a transformative practice, with affirmations to cultivate a grateful mindset and appreciate the blessings of motherhood.

8. Embracing Mindfulness: Mindfulness is the focus of this chapter, with affirmations guiding you to find calm, presence, and balance in the midst of the motherhood journey.

The book concludes with a final chapter that recaps the key concepts and affirmations covered throughout. It provides encouragement to integrate affirmations into your daily life, reminding you of the incredible journey of motherhood and self-growth.

"Affirmations Moms Actually Need" is more than just a book. It is a companion, offering support, inspiration, and guidance to help you embrace the joys, navigate the challenges, and nurture your well-being as a mom. Through its pages, you will find solace, strength, and the empowering reminders you need to thrive on your beautiful journey of motherhood.

Embracing Self-Care

A. **Understanding the importance of self-care for moms**

1. Exploring the misconceptions and guilt surrounding self-care

2. Recognizing the significance of self-care in maintaining overall well-being

3. Highlighting the positive impact of self-care on parenting and relationships

B. Identifying and addressing self-care needs

1. Reflecting on personal needs and desires as a mom

2. Understanding the different dimensions of self-care (physical, emotional, mental, and spiritual)

3. Developing strategies to prioritize and meet self-care needs

C. Affirmations for nurturing self-care routines

1. Affirmations for setting boundaries and saying no without guilt

2. Affirmations for making self-care a non-negotiable part of daily life

3. Affirmations for prioritizing self-care without feeling selfish

D. Practical self-care tips and activities

1. Exploring various self-care practices suitable for moms

2. Creating a personalized self-care plan

3. Incorporating self-care into busy schedules and adapting it to different stages of motherhood

E. Overcoming barriers to self-care

1. Addressing common obstacles and excuses for neglecting self-care

2. Strategies for overcoming guilt, time constraints, and societal expectations

3. Seeking support and building a community that values and encourages self-care

F. Self-compassion and self-care

1. Understanding the connection between self-compassion and self-care

2. Affirmations for cultivating self-compassion in the pursuit of self-care

3. Practicing self-forgiveness and embracing imperfections in the self-care journey

G. Creating a sustainable self-care routine

1. Establishing self-care habits that align with personal values and preferences

2. Exploring self-care rituals and practices that provide long-term benefits

3. Maintaining self-care as an ongoing commitment to personal well-being

H. Affirmations for self-care and motherhood

1. Affirmations for honoring personal needs alongside the demands of motherhood

2. Affirmations for embracing self-care as an act of love for oneself and one's family

3. Affirmations for finding balance and harmony through self-care practices

This chapter focuses on the crucial aspect of self-care for moms, highlighting its significance, addressing common barriers, and providing affirmations and practical tips to help moms prioritize and embrace self-care as an essential part of their lives. By nurturing their own well-being, moms can show up as their best selves for their families and experience greater joy, fulfillment, and resilience in their motherhood journey.

The significance of self-care for moms

Identifying and addressing self-care needs

To effectively practice self-care, it is crucial to identify and address your specific needs as a mom. Recognizing what nurtures and rejuvenates you allows you to create a tailored self-care routine that truly supports your well-being. Here are steps to help you identify and address your self-care needs:

1. Reflect on your needs: Take time for self-reflection and introspection. Consider what activities, experiences, or practices bring you joy, relaxation, and a sense of rejuvenation. Think about the things that make you feel nurtured, inspired, and fulfilled. This reflection helps you gain clarity about your unique self-care needs.

2. Consider the dimensions of self-care: Self-care encompasses various dimensions, including physical, emotional, mental, and spiritual well-being. Assess each dimension and identify areas where you may be neglecting self-care. For example, you may need physical self-care through exercise, emotional self-care through journaling or talking to a friend, mental self-care through engaging in a hobby or learning something new, and spiritual self-care through meditation or connecting with nature.

3. Prioritize self-care activities: Once you have identified your self-care needs, prioritize them. Determine which activities or practices are most important and feasible for you to incorporate into your routine. Remember that self-care

doesn't always have to be time-consuming or elaborate. Even small moments of self-care can have a significant impact on your well-being.

4. Create a self-care plan: Develop a self-care plan that aligns with your needs and priorities. Consider what self-care activities you can realistically integrate into your daily, weekly, or monthly routine. Be intentional about scheduling dedicated self-care time and committing to it. Your plan may include activities such as taking a relaxing bath, going for a walk, reading a book, practicing mindfulness, or engaging in creative pursuits.

5. Adapt self-care to different stages of motherhood: Recognize that your self-care needs may evolve as you go through different stages of motherhood. Be open to adjusting and adapting your self-care practices accordingly. What worked during the newborn phase may not be the same as your children grow older. Continuously reassess and modify your self-care plan to meet your evolving needs.

6. Seek support and communicate your needs: It's important to communicate your self-care needs to your partner, family, or friends. Seek their support in creating a nurturing environment that allows you to prioritize self-care. Share your self-care plan with them and ask for their understanding and assistance in honoring your self-care time.

Remember, identifying and addressing your self-care needs is an ongoing process. Be gentle with yourself and allow flexibility in your self-care routine. Adapt as needed, and remember that investing in your well-being is essential not just for you but also for your ability to be present and nurturing for your family.

Affirmations for nurturing self-care routines

Affirmations are powerful tools that can support and reinforce your commitment to self-care. By incorporating positive affirmations into your daily practice, you can strengthen your belief in the importance of self-care and cultivate a mindset that encourages and prioritizes self-nurturing. Here are some affirmations to help you nurture your self-care routines:

1. "I deserve to prioritize my self-care without guilt or hesitation."

2. "Taking care of myself is not selfish; it is an act of love towards myself and my family."

3. "My well-being matters, and I commit to making self-care a priority in my life."

4. "I am worthy of dedicated time and energy for self-care."

5. "I honor my needs and create space in my life for activities that bring me joy and rejuvenation."

6. "I release any guilt or judgment surrounding my self-care choices. I embrace them with love and acceptance."

7. "I listen to my body, mind, and heart, and provide them with the care they need."

8. "I give myself permission to rest, recharge, and replenish my energy."

9. "I nourish my soul by engaging in activities that bring me peace, inspiration, and happiness."

10. "I trust my intuition to guide me towards the self-care practices that serve me best."

11. "I create a self-care routine that suits my unique needs and supports my overall well-being."

12. "I set boundaries to protect my self-care time and honor my commitments to myself."

13. "I release the need to do it all and embrace the power of saying no when necessary."

14. "I am worthy of receiving support and assistance in caring for myself."

15. "I celebrate and appreciate the small moments of self-care in my day-to-day life."

16. "I release any self-imposed pressure to be perfect and embrace self-care as a journey, not a destination."

17. "I find joy in taking care of myself and embrace the positive impact it has on my well-being."

18. "I am grateful for the opportunity to prioritize my self-care and nurture my body, mind, and soul."

19. "I let go of any guilt associated with taking care of myself. My self-care is an investment in my overall happiness and fulfillment."

20. "I commit to making self-care an ongoing and non-negotiable part of my life."

Repeat these affirmations daily, either silently or out loud, and allow them to reaffirm your dedication to self-care. Let them serve as a reminder of your worthiness, your commitment to nurturing yourself, and the positive impact self-care has on your overall well-being as a mom.

Embracing Imperfections

A **. Understanding the beauty of imperfections**

1.Recognizing that perfection is an unattainable ideal

2. Understanding that imperfections are what make us unique and human

3. Embracing the beauty and authenticity that comes from embracing imperfections

B. Letting go of the need for perfection

1. Challenging unrealistic expectations and societal pressures

2. Releasing self-judgment and self-criticism

3. Cultivating self-acceptance and self-love as a foundation for embracing imperfections

C. Embracing vulnerability and authenticity

1. Embracing vulnerability as a strength and a pathway to genuine connection

2. Allowing yourself to be authentic and true to who you are

3. Recognizing that vulnerability and imperfections are part of the human experience

D. Practicing self-compassion and forgiveness

1. Offering yourself compassion and understanding when you make mistakes or fall short

2. Forgiving yourself for past mistakes and allowing yourself to move forward

3. Cultivating a mindset of self-compassion and forgiveness in all aspects of life

E. Celebrating growth and progress
   1. Recognizing and celebrating the growth and progress you have made on your journey

   2. Focusing on the small victories and milestones along the way

   3. Embracing the idea that growth and progress are more important than perfection

F. Embracing imperfections in motherhood
   1. Understanding that there is no such thing as a perfect mother

   2. Embracing the ups and downs of motherhood as part of the journey

   3. Finding joy and fulfillment in the imperfect but beautiful moments of motherhood

G. Affirmations for embracing imperfections
   1. Affirmations for letting go of perfection and embracing authenticity

   2. Affirmations for cultivating self-compassion and forgiveness

   3. Affirmations for finding joy and fulfillment in the imperfections of motherhood

This chapter focuses on the importance of embracing imperfections as a way to cultivate self-acceptance, authenticity, and growth. By letting go of the need for perfection and embracing vulnerability, self-compassion, and forgiveness, mothers can find joy and fulfillment in the imperfect but beautiful moments of motherhood.

Letting go of perfectionism and unrealistic expectations

Affirmations for setting boundaries

1. "I honor and respect my own needs by setting clear and healthy boundaries."

2. "Setting boundaries is an act of self-love and self-preservation."

3. "I have the right to prioritize my well-being by establishing boundaries that support my physical, emotional, and mental health."

4. "I release the need to please everyone and prioritize my own needs through firm and loving boundaries."

5. "I trust myself to communicate my boundaries with clarity, kindness, and assertiveness."

6. "I embrace the power of saying no when it aligns with my boundaries and supports my well-being."

7. "I am worthy of creating a safe space for myself by establishing and maintaining boundaries."

8. "Setting boundaries empowers me to maintain a healthy balance between my personal life and responsibilities."

9. "I release any guilt or fear associated with setting boundaries, knowing that they are essential for my self-care and happiness."

10. "I am deserving of respect, and setting boundaries teaches others how to treat me."

11. "I trust my intuition to guide me in setting boundaries that honor my values and priorities."

12. "I communicate my boundaries clearly and confidently, knowing that I have the right to protect my time, energy, and emotional well-being."

13. "I attract and surround myself with people who respect and honor my boundaries."

14. "I let go of the need to explain or justify my boundaries. They are valid simply because they are mine."

15. "I embrace the power of boundaries as a way to foster healthy and fulfilling relationships."

16. "Setting boundaries allows me to create space for self-care and to recharge my energy."

17. "I release any guilt or obligation to please others at the expense of my own well-being."

18. "I prioritize self-respect and self-care by setting and upholding clear boundaries."

19. "I choose to create a harmonious and balanced life by setting boundaries that support my overall well-being."

20. "I have the strength and courage to set and maintain boundaries that serve my highest good."

Repeat these affirmations regularly, internalizing their empowering messages. Allow them to guide you in setting and upholding boundaries that honor your needs, protect your well-being, and create a healthier and more fulfilling life. Remember, setting boundaries is an act of self-care and self-respect that ultimately benefits both you and your relationships.

Affirmations for guilt-free self-care

1. "I release any guilt associated with taking time for myself. I deserve and need guilt-free self-care."

2. "Self-care is not selfish; it is necessary for my well-being. I give myself permission to prioritize it without guilt."

3. "I let go of the belief that I should always put others' needs before my own. I am worthy of guilt-free self-care."

4. "My self-care is a gift to myself and those around me. I release any guilt and fully embrace its positive impact."

5. "I am allowed to prioritize my own needs and well-being. Guilt has no place in my self-care journey."

6. "I deserve to recharge and nurture myself without feeling guilty. I release the need to justify self-care."

7. "I choose to be kind to myself and let go of any guilt that arises when I practice self-care."

8. "Guilt has no power over my self-care decisions. I trust myself to know what I need and honor it guilt-free."

9. "I am a better mom when I prioritize self-care. I release guilt and fully embrace the benefits it brings to myself and my family."

10. "I deserve joy, relaxation, and rejuvenation. Guilt cannot take away my right to guilt-free self-care."

11. "My self-care is an investment in my overall happiness and well-being. I release guilt and embrace the positive impact it has on my life."

12. "Guilt does not serve me. I choose to let it go and fully enjoy guilt-free self-care."

13. "I give myself permission to take care of myself without guilt or apology. My self-care is valid and necessary."

14. "I release the belief that I need to earn or justify self-care. I am worthy of guilt-free self-care simply because I exist."

15. "I am a deserving and loving mother, and guilt has no place in my self-care routine."

16. "Guilt is not a helpful emotion when it comes to self-care. I choose to let go of guilt and embrace self-nurturing wholeheartedly."

17. "I release any societal expectations or judgment that causes me to feel guilty about self-care. My well-being matters."

18. "I trust my instincts and intuition when it comes to self-care. I release guilt and listen to what my mind and body truly need."

19. "Guilt is a choice, and I choose to release it. I fully embrace guilt-free self-care with love and acceptance."

20. "I am worthy of guilt-free self-care, and I give myself permission to prioritize it unapologetically."

Repeat these affirmations regularly to reprogram your mindset and let go of any guilt associated with self-care. Embrace the truth that guilt-free self-care is not only beneficial but essential for your well-being as a mom. Remember, taking care of yourself is a beautiful act of self-love that enhances your ability to show up as the best version of yourself for your family.

Affirmations for prioritizing well-being

1. "My well-being is a priority in my life, and I commit to nurturing it with love and intention."

2. "I choose to prioritize my well-being because I understand that it is the foundation for a fulfilling life."

3. "I deserve to invest time and energy into my well-being. I give myself permission to make it a top priority."

4. "I release any guilt or hesitation in putting my well-being first. I know that by prioritizing myself, I can better serve others."

5. "My well-being matters, and I honor it by consciously choosing actions and habits that support my physical, mental, and emotional health."

6. "I am worthy of living a life of well-being and balance. I choose to make decisions that align with my holistic wellness."

7. "Prioritizing my well-being is an act of self-love and self-respect. I am committed to taking care of myself."

8. "I release the belief that putting others' needs before mine is noble. I understand that by prioritizing my well-being, I can show up as my best self."

9. "I trust myself to make choices that prioritize my well-being. I listen to my body, mind, and heart to guide me on this path."

10. "I am deserving of a life that is balanced, healthy, and fulfilling. I choose to prioritize my well-being to create that reality."

11. "I embrace the power of self-care and healthy boundaries in prioritizing my well-being. I honor my needs without apology."

12. "I let go of any societal expectations that undermine my well-being. I define my own path and prioritize what serves me best."

13. "I am not selfish for prioritizing my well-being. By taking care of myself, I am better able to care for others."

14. "My well-being is a lifelong journey, and I am committed to continually nurturing and prioritizing it."

15. "I release the need for perfection in prioritizing my well-being. Progress and self-care efforts are what truly matter."

16. "I am capable of creating a balanced life that allows me to prioritize my well-being alongside my responsibilities."

17. "I make choices that support my well-being because I value myself and my overall quality of life."

18. "I release any guilt associated with self-care and prioritizing my well-being. I trust that I am deserving and worthy."

19. "I choose to listen to my intuition and honor my well-being needs. I know that by doing so, I am living authentically."

20. "I am the guardian of my well-being, and I embrace the responsibility of prioritizing it for a life of joy, fulfillment, and balance."

Repeat these affirmations regularly to reinforce your commitment to prioritizing your well-being. Let them guide you in making choices and taking actions that align with your holistic wellness. Remember, by prioritizing your well-being, you create a foundation for a healthier, happier, and more fulfilling life for yourself and those around you.

Overcoming Mom Guilt

A. **Understanding the impact of mom guilt**

  1.Exploring the common experience of mom guilt and its emotional toll

  2. Recognizing the negative effects of mom guilt on self-esteem and well-being

  3. Understanding that mom guilt is not productive or beneficial

B. Identifying the sources of mom guilt

  1. Exploring societal expectations and pressures on motherhood

  2. Examining personal beliefs and internalized expectations that contribute to mom guilt

  3. Recognizing the influence of comparison and judgment in triggering mom guilt

C. Challenging and reframing mom guilt

  1. Becoming aware of negative self-talk and thoughts associated with mom guilt

  2. Recognizing that self-compassion and self-forgiveness are essential in overcoming mom guilt

  3. Reframing mom guilt as an opportunity for growth and learning rather than a sign of failure

D. Cultivating self-acceptance and self-compassion

1. Embracing imperfections and understanding that no one is a perfect mom

2. Practicing self-compassion by treating oneself with kindness, understanding, and forgiveness

3. Celebrating personal accomplishments and acknowledging the effort put into motherhood

E. Building a support network

1. Seeking connection with other moms who understand the challenges of motherhood

2. Sharing experiences and supporting each other in overcoming mom guilt

3. Seeking professional help if mom guilt becomes overwhelming or detrimental to mental well-being

F. Letting go of unrealistic expectations

1. Identifying and challenging unrealistic expectations placed on oneself as a mom

2. Embracing a mindset of flexibility and adaptability in motherhood

3. Focusing on the present moment and letting go of past mistakes or regrets

G. Affirmations for releasing mom guilt

1. Affirmations for embracing self-acceptance and letting go of perfectionism

2. Affirmations for practicing self-compassion and forgiveness in the face of mom guilt

3. Affirmations for embracing the joys and accomplishments of motherhood without guilt

H. Strategies for moving forward

1. Developing a gratitude practice to shift focus from guilt to appreciation

2. Setting realistic expectations and prioritizing self-care to prevent mom guilt

3. Creating a positive and supportive environment that celebrates individual parenting journeys

This chapter is dedicated to exploring the common experience of mom guilt, understanding its impact, and providing strategies to overcome it. By challenging negative thoughts, practicing self-compassion, and embracing self-acceptance, moms can release the burden of mom guilt and experience greater joy, confidence, and fulfillment in their journey of motherhood.

Understanding the origins and effects of mom guilt

Mom guilt is a pervasive and often overwhelming emotion that many mothers experience. It stems from the belief that we are falling short or failing in some aspect of our mothering responsibilities. Understanding the origins and effects of mom guilt can help us navigate and overcome its impact on our well-being.

1. Societal expectations and external pressures: Society often imposes unrealistic expectations on mothers, perpetuating the idea of a "perfect" mom who effortlessly balances all aspects of her life. These societal pressures can contribute to feelings of guilt when we perceive ourselves as not meeting these impossible standards.

2. Internalized beliefs and comparisons: As mothers, we may internalize beliefs about what it means to be a "good" mom, often comparing ourselves to others. Constant comparisons and self-judgment can lead to a sense of guilt if we feel we are not measuring up to the perceived standards set by others.

3. Emotional impact: Mom guilt can have significant emotional effects. It can lead to feelings of inadequacy, self-doubt, and shame. It can erode our self-esteem and create a constant state of worry and self-criticism. These emotional burdens can negatively impact our mental well-being and overall enjoyment of motherhood.

4. Interference with self-care and well-being: Mom guilt often prevents mothers from prioritizing their own needs and engaging in self-care activities. The belief that self-care is selfish can lead to neglecting our own well-being, resulting in exhaustion, burnout, and a diminished ability to care for our families effectively.

5. Strained relationships: Mom guilt can strain relationships, as it can lead to feelings of resentment or frustration towards loved ones. It may also create a barrier to seeking help or support, as we may feel guilty or ashamed for needing assistance.

Recognizing the origins and effects of mom guilt is the first step in overcoming its grip on our lives. By challenging unrealistic expectations, practicing self-compassion, and fostering a supportive environment, we can free ourselves from the burden of mom guilt and cultivate a healthier, more fulfilling experience of motherhood.

Cultivating self-compassion and self-forgiveness

C ultivating self-compassion and self-forgiveness is crucial in overcoming mom guilt and nurturing our well-being as mothers. These practices allow us to embrace our imperfections, acknowledge our efforts, and offer ourselves the same kindness and understanding we would extend to others. Here are strategies for cultivating self-compassion and self-forgiveness:

1. Practice self-awareness: Notice and acknowledge when mom guilt arises. Be aware of the self-critical thoughts and judgments that accompany it. Recognize that these thoughts are not helpful or productive.

2. Challenge negative self-talk: Counteract self-critical thoughts with compassionate and understanding statements. Remind yourself that no one is perfect, and motherhood is a learning journey filled with ups and downs.

3. Embrace imperfection: Accept that making mistakes and experiencing challenges are part of being a mother. Embrace imperfection as an opportunity for growth and learning, rather than a reflection of your worth as a mom.

4. Treat yourself with kindness: Offer yourself the same kindness and compassion you would offer a dear friend. Be gentle with yourself when things don't go as planned or when you feel overwhelmed. Remind yourself that you are doing

your best.

5. Practice self-forgiveness: Forgive yourself for past mistakes or perceived short-comings. Recognize that holding onto guilt and self-blame only hinders your growth and well-being. Release the past and focus on the present moment.

6. Engage in self-care: Prioritize self-care activities that nurture your physical, emotional, and mental well-being. Taking time for self-care replenishes your energy and fosters self-compassion.

7. Seek support: Reach out to trusted friends, family members, or support groups who understand the challenges of motherhood. Share your struggles and feelings of guilt. Their empathy and encouragement can help you cultivate self-compassion and perspective.

8. Practice mindfulness: Engage in mindfulness techniques, such as deep breathing, meditation, or body scans, to cultivate self-awareness and create space for self-compassion. Mindfulness can help you observe your thoughts and emotions without judgment.

9. Release perfectionism: Let go of the need to be a perfect mom. Embrace the idea that good enough is truly enough. Give yourself permission to make mistakes and learn from them, knowing that they are part of the journey.

10. Celebrate your efforts: Acknowledge and celebrate the love, care, and effort you put into being a mom. Recognize that your dedication and commitment to your family are valuable and worthy of appreciation.

Remember, self-compassion and self-forgiveness are ongoing practices. Be patient with yourself and offer kindness and understanding even during difficult times. By cultivating self-compassion and self-forgiveness, you can free yourself from the grip of mom guilt and create a nurturing and supportive environment for yourself and your family.

Affirmations for releasing mom guilt

Affirmations can be powerful tools to help release mom guilt and cultivate a mindset of self-acceptance and self-love. Repeat these affirmations regularly to reinforce positive beliefs and overcome feelings of guilt:

1. "I release any guilt that weighs me down. I am doing my best as a mom."

2. "I am deserving of love, compassion, and forgiveness, including from myself."

3. "I let go of comparing myself to others. I embrace my unique journey as a mom."

4. "I am allowed to prioritize my well-being without guilt. Taking care of myself makes me a better mom."

5. "I release the need for perfection. I am a loving and capable mom despite my imperfections."

6. "I forgive myself for past mistakes. I am growing and learning every day."

7. "I trust my instincts as a mom. I make choices based on what I believe is best for my family."

8. "I release the need to please everyone. My worth as a mom is not determined by the opinions of others."

9. "I am allowed to ask for help when I need it. Seeking support is a sign of strength, not weakness."

10. "I celebrate my efforts and accomplishments as a mom, no matter how small they may seem."

11. "I am allowed to set boundaries and say no without guilt. My well-being matters."

12. "I release the burden of mom guilt and embrace self-compassion in its place."

13. "I choose to focus on the positive moments and experiences in motherhood, letting go of guilt over the rest."

14. "I am doing enough for my children. I provide them with love, care, and support to the best of my abilities."

15. "I release the need to control every aspect of motherhood. I trust in the process and allow room for spontaneity and growth."

16. "I give myself permission to make mistakes and learn from them. I am constantly evolving as a mom."

17. "I am worthy of happiness and fulfillment beyond motherhood. Pursuing my own dreams and passions is not selfish."

18. "I choose to focus on the present moment and let go of guilt over the past. Each day is an opportunity for growth and connection."

19. "I am grateful for the love and bond I share with my children. My presence and love are more important than perfection."

20. "I embrace the joy and beauty of motherhood without guilt. I am enough exactly as I am."

Repeat these affirmations with conviction and belief in your inherent worth as a mom. Allow them to transform your mindset and release the grip of mom guilt, paving the way for greater self-acceptance, joy, and fulfillment in your journey of motherhood.

Affirmations for accepting imperfections

1. "I embrace my imperfections as a beautiful part of my journey as a mom."

2. "I release the need to be perfect and instead celebrate my unique qualities and strengths."

3. "I accept that mistakes are opportunities for growth and learning in my role as a mom."

4. "I am allowed to make mistakes and still be a loving and capable mom."

5. "I let go of the unrealistic expectations of perfection and embrace my authentic self."

6. "I accept that perfection is unattainable and find beauty in the messy and imperfect moments of motherhood."

7. "I am worthy of love and acceptance, regardless of any perceived flaws or mistakes."

8. "I celebrate the growth and progress I have made as a mom, even in the face of imperfection."

9. "I release the need to compare myself to others. I am unique, and my imperfections make me who I am."

10. "I choose self-compassion over self-criticism when faced with imperfections or challenges."

11. "I accept that I am doing my best with the knowledge and resources I have at this moment."

12. "I am deserving of grace and understanding when I fall short of my own expectations."

13. "I appreciate the lessons and wisdom gained from my imperfections. They contribute to my personal growth and resilience."

14. "I am grateful for the opportunity to learn from my mistakes and become a better mom each day."

15. "I embrace the imperfect moments with my children, knowing that they contribute to our authentic connection and bond."

16. "I let go of the need to control every aspect of motherhood and instead trust in the process."

17. "I accept that I am a work in progress, and that is okay. I am constantly growing and evolving as a mom."

18. "I release the pressure to be perfect and instead focus on being present and loving for my children."

19. "I choose self-acceptance and self-love, embracing my imperfections as a part of my unique story."

20. "I am enough, exactly as I am. My imperfections do not define my worth as a mom."

Repeat these affirmations with kindness and acceptance, embracing the beauty of imperfection in your journey as a mom. Allow them to shift your perspective and cultivate a sense of self-acceptance, love, and appreciation for all that you are as a mom, imperfections and all.

Affirmations for acknowledging personal needs

1. Affirmations for acknowledging personal needs

2. "My needs are valid, and I give myself permission to prioritize them."

3. "I am worthy of having my personal needs met, just as I meet the needs of others."

4. "I deserve to take care of myself and honor my own well-being."

5. "I listen to my body, mind, and heart, and I honor their signals for rest, nourishment, and self-care."

6. "I embrace the importance of self-care and recognize that it is essential for my overall happiness and fulfillment."

7. "I release any guilt or hesitation in acknowledging and expressing my personal needs."

8. "I trust my instincts in recognizing and responding to my personal needs."

9. "I am deserving of time and space to recharge, rejuvenate, and focus on my own growth and well-being."

10. "I prioritize self-care and self-nurturing as essential components of a balanced and fulfilling life."

11. "I value myself enough to acknowledge and honor my personal boundaries and limitations."

12. "I give myself permission to say no when necessary and protect my time and energy."

13. "I am deserving of support and assistance in meeting my personal needs. Asking for help is a sign of strength, not weakness."

14. "I am proactive in seeking ways to fulfill my personal needs and create a life that aligns with my values and desires."

15. "I let go of any guilt or obligation to constantly put others' needs before my own. Taking care of myself allows me to show up fully for others."

16. "I trust that by acknowledging and meeting my personal needs, I am cultivating a foundation of strength and resilience."

17. "I am deserving of joy, fulfillment, and self-expression. I prioritize activities and experiences that nourish my soul."

18. "I honor my personal needs without judgment or comparison. Each person's needs are unique and valid."

19. "I release the belief that putting myself last is a virtue. I understand that self-care is a necessary investment in my well-being."

20. "I am allowed to create boundaries that protect my personal needs and ensure a healthy balance in my life."

21. "I commit to honoring and meeting my personal needs unapologetically, knowing that doing so enhances my overall quality of life."

Repeat these affirmations regularly to reinforce the importance of acknowledging and prioritizing your personal needs. Embrace the belief that taking care of yourself is not selfish, but rather an act of self-love and self-preservation. By recognizing and meeting your personal needs, you create a strong foundation for a balanced, fulfilling, and joyful life.

Affirmations for embracing the joys of motherhood

1. "I embrace the precious moments and joys of motherhood with an open heart and gratitude."

2. "I find joy in the everyday moments, knowing that they create cherished memories."

3. "I am grateful for the opportunity to experience the unconditional love and connection that comes with being a mother."

4. "I celebrate the growth, milestones, and achievements of my children, finding joy in their accomplishments."

5. "I treasure the laughter, hugs, and smiles shared with my children, knowing that they bring immense happiness."

6. "I choose to focus on the positive aspects of motherhood, allowing them to overshadow any challenges I may face."

7. "I find joy in the simple pleasures of motherhood, savoring the small moments that bring happiness and contentment."

8. "I embrace the unique bond I share with my children, cherishing the love and connection that flows between us."

9. "I appreciate the beauty of watching my children grow and learn, finding fulfillment in witnessing their journey."

10. "I create space for fun and playfulness in my interactions with my children, allowing joy to permeate our lives."

11. "I let go of perfectionism and embrace the imperfect moments, finding joy in the authenticity of motherhood."

12. "I find joy in nurturing and caring for my children, knowing that my love and support make a positive difference in their lives."

13. "I am grateful for the lessons and growth that motherhood brings, finding joy in the opportunities for personal development."

14. "I take time to pause and appreciate the beauty of the present moment, fully embracing the joys that motherhood offers."

15. "I find joy in creating traditions and memories with my children, cherishing the experiences we share together."

16. "I choose to approach motherhood with a sense of wonder and curiosity, finding joy in the exploration and discovery alongside my children."

17. "I release any guilt or comparison that detracts from my joy as a mother. I celebrate my unique journey and experiences."

18. "I am deserving of joy and happiness as a mother. I allow myself to fully experience and embrace the joys that come my way."

19. "I find fulfillment in the role of a mother, appreciating the significance and impact I have on my children's lives."

20. "I am grateful for the privilege of being a mother, and I embrace the abundant joys that come with this role."

Repeat these affirmations with a genuine sense of joy and appreciation for the joys of motherhood. Let them remind you to savor the precious moments, embrace the love and connection, and find fulfillment in the journey of being a mother. By focusing on the joys, you create a positive and nurturing environment for yourself and your children, enhancing the richness and beauty of your motherhood experience.

Building Resilience

A. **Understanding the concept of resilience**

1.Defining resilience and its relevance in the context of motherhood

2. Recognizing the importance of resilience in navigating challenges and setbacks

3. Understanding that resilience is a skill that can be developed and strengthened

B. Cultivating a positive mindset

1. Shifting focus towards gratitude and positive thinking

2. Challenging negative self-talk and reframing setbacks as opportunities for growth

3. Embracing optimism and maintaining a hopeful outlook

C. Practicing self-care for emotional well-being

1. Prioritizing self-care activities that nurture mental and emotional health

2. Engaging in stress-reducing practices such as meditation, deep breathing, or journaling

3. Seeking professional support when needed to address and process emotions

D. Building a support network

1. Nurturing relationships with trusted friends, family members, or support

groups

2. Seeking emotional support and sharing experiences with others who understand the challenges of motherhood

3. Collaborating with others to share responsibilities and provide mutual support

E. Developing coping strategies for stress and overwhelm
1. Identifying triggers and sources of stress

2. Implementing effective coping mechanisms such as time management, boundary-setting, and relaxation techniques

3. Seeking balance and practicing self-compassion when faced with overwhelming situations

F. Enhancing problem-solving and decision-making skills
1. Developing effective problem-solving strategies to tackle challenges

2. Improving decision-making skills by considering options, weighing pros and cons, and trusting intuition

3. Embracing flexibility and adaptability when unforeseen circumstances arise

G. Embracing change and embracing growth
1. Recognizing that change is inevitable in motherhood and embracing it as an opportunity for personal growth

2. Cultivating a mindset of resilience by adapting to new situations and embracing the learning process

3. Celebrating personal growth and acknowledging accomplishments along the journey

H. Affirmations for building resilience
1. Affirmations for developing a positive mindset and reframing challenges

2. Affirmations for practicing self-care and nurturing emotional well-being

3. Affirmations for embracing change, growth, and resilience in motherhood

This chapter focuses on building resilience as a mother, recognizing the importance of developing coping strategies, seeking support, and cultivating a positive mindset. By strengthening resilience, moms can navigate challenges, bounce back from setbacks, and thrive amidst the demands of motherhood.

Recognizing and managing stress and overwhelm

1. Understanding stress triggers: Recognize the situations, responsibilities, or thoughts that contribute to your stress and overwhelm. Identifying these triggers can help you proactively manage them.

2. Prioritizing self-care: Make self-care a non-negotiable part of your routine. Engage in activities that rejuvenate and relax you, such as exercise, meditation, reading, or pursuing hobbies. Prioritizing self-care replenishes your energy and resilience.

3. Setting boundaries: Establish clear boundaries to protect your time, energy, and emotional well-being. Learn to say no to commitments that do not align with your priorities or add unnecessary stress to your life. Setting boundaries allows you to focus on what truly matters.

4. Seeking support: Reach out to trusted friends, family, or support groups who can provide emotional support and understanding. Share your feelings and experiences, and allow others to offer assistance and perspective. Remember, asking for help is a sign of strength, not weakness.

5. Practicing stress-reducing techniques: Engage in stress-reducing practices that

work for you, such as deep breathing exercises, mindfulness meditation, progressive muscle relaxation, or journaling. These techniques help calm your mind, reduce stress levels, and promote a sense of well-being.

6. Time management: Prioritize and organize your tasks to effectively manage your time. Break larger tasks into smaller, more manageable steps and create a schedule or to-do list to stay organized. Be realistic about what you can accomplish in a given time frame.

7. Practicing self-compassion: Be kind and understanding towards yourself when you feel overwhelmed. Treat yourself with the same compassion and support you would offer a friend. Recognize that it's okay to ask for help and take breaks when needed.

8. Finding healthy outlets for stress: Engage in activities that help you release stress and tension, such as exercising, listening to music, practicing yoga, or spending time in nature. Find healthy outlets that provide a sense of relaxation and rejuvenation.

9. Engaging in positive self-talk: Challenge negative thoughts and replace them with positive affirmations. Remind yourself of your strengths, capabilities, and past successes. Focus on what you have accomplished rather than what you haven't.

10. Seeking professional help if needed: If stress and overwhelm become persistent and interfere with your daily life, consider seeking professional support. A therapist or counselor can provide guidance, coping strategies, and a safe space to process your emotions.

Remember, managing stress and overwhelm is an ongoing practice. Be patient with yourself and allow room for self-care and self-compassion. By recognizing and actively managing stress, you can create a healthier and more balanced life as a mom.

Strengthening mental and emotional resilience

1. Cultivating self-awareness: Develop an understanding of your thoughts, emotions, and reactions. Pay attention to how you perceive and interpret situations, as this awareness allows you to consciously choose more resilient perspectives.

2. Practicing gratitude: Regularly express gratitude for the positive aspects of your life, even during challenging times. Focusing on gratitude can shift your mindset towards resilience and increase your ability to bounce back from adversity.

3. Developing a growth mindset: Embrace the belief that challenges and setbacks are opportunities for growth and learning. Instead of viewing failures as permanent, see them as stepping stones towards improvement and development.

4. Building a support network: Surround yourself with supportive and positive individuals who uplift and encourage you. Seek out relationships that provide emotional support and a sense of belonging. A strong support network can bolster your resilience.

5. Nurturing self-care practices: Engage in activities that promote self-care and emotional well-being. This can include exercise, mindfulness practices, creative outlets, or engaging in hobbies that bring you joy and relaxation. Taking care of

yourself strengthens your resilience.

6. Developing problem-solving skills: Enhance your ability to tackle challenges by developing effective problem-solving strategies. Break down problems into smaller, manageable steps, explore various solutions, and seek different perspectives when needed.

7. Cultivating flexibility and adaptability: Embrace change as a natural part of life and motherhood. Develop the ability to adapt to new situations and adjust your expectations accordingly. Flexibility allows you to navigate challenges with greater ease and resilience.

8. Practicing self-compassion: Treat yourself with kindness and understanding during difficult times. Recognize that you are doing the best you can and that mistakes and setbacks are part of the journey. Embrace self-compassion as a nurturing foundation for resilience.

9. Developing positive coping strategies: Identify healthy coping mechanisms that help you manage stress and adversity. This can include deep breathing exercises, journaling, seeking professional support, or engaging in relaxation techniques. Find strategies that work best for you.

10. Embracing self-belief: Cultivate a positive belief in your own capabilities and strengths. Remind yourself of past accomplishments and successes. Trust in your ability to overcome challenges and persevere in the face of adversity.

11. Embracing self-reflection: Regularly engage in self-reflection to gain insights into your patterns, behaviors, and thoughts. This allows you to make adjustments, learn from experiences, and strengthen your resilience over time.

12. Embracing a positive perspective: Focus on the possibilities, opportunities, and potential for growth that arise from challenges. Embrace a positive outlook that allows you to see setbacks as temporary and the potential for positive change.

Remember that building mental and emotional resilience is a journey. Consistently practice these strategies, remain patient with yourself, and celebrate the progress you make along the way. By strengthening your resilience, you empower yourself to navigate the ups and downs of motherhood with greater confidence and well-being.

Affirmations for resilience and inner strength

Affirmations for coping with challenging moments

Affirmations for adapting to change

1. "I embrace change with an open mind and a willingness to learn and grow."

2. "I am flexible and adaptable, capable of adjusting to new circumstances with ease."

3. "Change is an opportunity for personal growth, and I welcome it with excitement and curiosity."

4. "I trust in my ability to navigate and embrace change with grace and resilience."

5. "I release resistance to change and instead embrace the possibilities it brings."

6. "I am open to new experiences and perspectives that come with change."

7. "I adapt to change with resilience and find strength in the process."

8. "Change allows me to discover new strengths and capabilities within myself."

9. "I flow with the changes in life, knowing that they lead me to greater opportunities and personal evolution."

10. "I let go of the need for control and embrace the natural ebb and flow of life."

11. "Change brings me growth and expansion, and I welcome it as a catalyst for positive transformation."

12. "I find peace in the midst of change, knowing that I have the inner stability to navigate through it."

13. "I release fear of the unknown and trust that change brings new beginnings and possibilities."

14. "I am resilient in the face of change, adapting and thriving in new environments and circumstances."

15. "I embrace change as a chance to redefine myself and create a life aligned with my true desires."

16. "Change challenges me to step out of my comfort zone and discover new strengths and potentials."

17. "I am open to the lessons and growth that change brings, knowing that it helps me evolve into the best version of myself."

18. "I have the power to create positive change in my life and embrace the opportunities that come my way."

19. "I trust in the journey of life and have faith that everything happens for my highest good."

20. "I am resilient, adaptable, and fully capable of embracing and thriving in the face of change."

Repeat these affirmations to reinforce your mindset of adaptability and resilience when facing change. Embrace change as a natural part of life and a catalyst for personal growth and transformation. With an open and flexible mindset, you can navigate changes with grace and confidence, embracing the opportunities that they bring.

Affirmations for finding balance amidst chaos

1. "I create a calm and centered space within myself, even amidst chaos."

2. "I trust in my ability to find balance and harmony in the midst of life's challenges."

3. "I prioritize self-care and make time for activities that restore my sense of balance."

4. "I release the need for perfection and embrace the beauty of finding balance in imperfect circumstances."

5. "I am in control of how I respond to chaos, and I choose to respond with grace and calmness."

6. "I trust in my inner wisdom to guide me towards decisions and actions that restore balance."

7. "I find peace in the present moment, anchoring myself in the here and now amidst chaos."

8. "I prioritize and manage my time effectively to create a sense of balance in my

daily life."

9. "I release overwhelm and invite a sense of ease and flow into my experience."

10. "I create boundaries to protect my time, energy, and well-being, fostering a sense of balance."

11. "I release the need to control every aspect of chaos and instead surrender to the process."

12. "I cultivate a mindset of flexibility and adaptability, allowing me to find balance amidst changing circumstances."

13. "I nurture my mind, body, and spirit, knowing that holistic well-being contributes to a sense of balance."

14. "I trust that even in the midst of chaos, I can find moments of peace and tranquility."

15. "I prioritize self-reflection and self-care, knowing that they are essential for finding and maintaining balance."

16. "I let go of what no longer serves me and create space for what brings me joy, peace, and balance."

17. "I embrace simplicity and focus on what truly matters, finding balance amidst the noise of life."

18. "I trust in my ability to find creative solutions and make choices that restore balance."

19. "I practice patience and compassion with myself and others as I navigate through chaotic times."

20. "I am a pillar of stability and calmness amidst chaos, radiating peace to those around me."

Repeat these affirmations to anchor yourself in a sense of balance amidst chaos. Embrace the power within you to find equilibrium, prioritize self-care, and make choices that align with your well-being. By maintaining a sense of balance, you can navigate through chaotic times with grace, resilience, and inner harmony.

Embracing Imperfections

A. **Understanding the beauty of imperfections**

1. Recognizing that perfection is an unattainable ideal

2. Understanding that imperfections are what make us unique and human

3. Embracing the beauty and authenticity that comes from embracing imperfections

B. Letting go of the need for perfection

1. Challenging unrealistic expectations and societal pressures

2. Releasing self-judgment and self-criticism

3. Cultivating self-acceptance and self-love as a foundation for embracing imperfections

C. Embracing vulnerability and authenticity

1. Embracing vulnerability as a strength and a pathway to genuine connection

2. Allowing yourself to be authentic and true to who you are

3. Recognizing that vulnerability and imperfections are part of the human experience

D. Practicing self-compassion and forgiveness

1. Offering yourself compassion and understanding when you make mistakes or fall short

2. Forgiving yourself for past mistakes and allowing yourself to move forward

3. Cultivating a mindset of self-compassion and forgiveness in all aspects of life

E. Celebrating growth and progress

1. Recognizing and celebrating the growth and progress you have made on your journey

2. Focusing on the small victories and milestones along the way

3. Embracing the idea that growth and progress are more important than perfection

F. Embracing imperfections in motherhood

1. Understanding that there is no such thing as a perfect mother

2. Embracing the ups and downs of motherhood as part of the journey

3. Finding joy and fulfillment in the imperfect but beautiful moments of motherhood

G. Affirmations for embracing imperfections

1. Affirmations for letting go of perfection and embracing authenticity

2. Affirmations for cultivating self-compassion and forgiveness

3. Affirmations for finding joy and fulfillment in the imperfections of motherhood

This chapter focuses on the importance of embracing imperfections as a way to cultivate self-acceptance, authenticity, and growth. By letting go of the need for perfection and embracing vulnerability, self-compassion, and forgiveness, mothers can find joy and fulfillment in the imperfect but beautiful moments of motherhood.

Letting go of perfectionism and unrealistic expectations

1. "I release the need for perfection and embrace the beauty of my imperfections."

2. "I let go of unrealistic expectations and instead focus on progress and growth."

3. "I am worthy and deserving of love and acceptance, regardless of achieving perfection."

4. "I embrace the idea that mistakes and imperfections are opportunities for learning and growth."

5. "I release the pressure to be perfect and allow myself to be authentically me."

6. "I recognize that perfection is an illusion, and I choose to embrace my uniqueness."

7. "I let go of comparing myself to others and instead focus on my own journey and progress."

8. "I accept that life is a series of beautiful imperfections, and I find joy in the messy moments."

9. "I celebrate my efforts and accomplishments, no matter how small they may seem."

10. "I value progress over perfection and appreciate the growth I experience along the way."

11. "I give myself permission to make mistakes and learn from them without judgment."

12. "I release the need for external validation and find validation within myself."

13. "I embrace the freedom that comes with letting go of perfectionism and embracing imperfection."

14. "I choose to focus on self-compassion and self-acceptance rather than seeking perfection."

15. "I allow room for spontaneity and mistakes, knowing that they often lead to unexpected joys and discoveries."

16. "I find beauty and strength in my vulnerability and imperfections."

17. "I accept that life is a continuous journey of growth, and perfection is not a requirement for happiness."

18. "I embrace the unique qualities and quirks that make me who I am."

19. "I let go of the need to control every outcome and instead trust in the natural flow of life."

20. "I am enough as I am, imperfections and all. I choose to love and accept myself fully."

Repeat these affirmations regularly to reinforce the practice of letting go of perfectionism and embracing the beauty of imperfections. By shifting your mindset and embracing self-acceptance, you can create a more fulfilling and joyful journey as a mom, free from the burdens of unrealistic expectations.

Celebrating the beauty of imperfections

1. "I celebrate the unique qualities and imperfections that make me beautifully human."

2. "I find beauty in the imperfect moments of my journey and embrace them as part of my story."

3. "I appreciate the authenticity that comes from embracing my imperfections."

4. "I choose to see imperfections as opportunities for growth, learning, and self-discovery."

5. "I celebrate the beauty of imperfections in myself and others, knowing they are what make us truly special."

6. "I find joy in the imperfect but genuine connections I share with others."

7. "I embrace imperfections as reminders of our shared humanity and the richness of life."

8. "I celebrate the beauty of imperfections as they add depth, character, and uniqueness to my life."

9. "I release the need for perfection and instead focus on embracing the imperfect beauty around me."

10. "I find peace and acceptance in celebrating the beauty of imperfections, both in myself and in the world."

11. "I choose to see imperfections as opportunities for creativity and innovation."

12. "I celebrate my own growth and progress, even when it comes with stumbling and learning along the way."

13. "I appreciate the lessons that imperfections teach me, allowing me to become a better version of myself."

14. "I find beauty in the imperfect but genuine moments shared with my loved ones."

15. "I celebrate the uniqueness of my journey, knowing that imperfections contribute to its richness and authenticity."

16. "I let go of the need for external validation and instead focus on self-acceptance and self-love."

17. "I choose to see imperfections as blessings in disguise, guiding me towards new perspectives and opportunities."

18. "I celebrate the growth and resilience that come from embracing imperfections with grace and kindness."

19. "I appreciate the imperfections in nature, art, and life, finding inspiration in their inherent beauty."

20. "I celebrate the beauty of imperfections by embracing the freedom and joy that comes with accepting myself unconditionally."

Repeat these affirmations with gratitude and appreciation for the beauty of imperfections. Celebrate the uniqueness and authenticity that imperfections bring to your life, and allow them to inspire growth, self-acceptance, and a deeper appreciation for the imperfectly beautiful moments in motherhood and beyond.

Affirmations for embracing self-acceptance

1. "I accept myself unconditionally, knowing that I am deserving of love and respect."

2. "I embrace my strengths, weaknesses, and everything in between, for they make me who I am."

3. "I release the need to compare myself to others and instead focus on my own unique journey."

4. "I am enough just as I am, and I accept myself fully, flaws and all."

5. "I choose to love and accept myself for who I am, recognizing my inherent worthiness."

6. "I let go of the need for external validation and find validation within myself."

7. "I honor my feelings, thoughts, and experiences, allowing myself to be authentic and true."

8. "I embrace self-compassion and kindness, knowing that I am deserving of gentleness and understanding."

9. "I celebrate my individuality and uniqueness, recognizing that it is a gift to the world."

10. "I release self-judgment and criticism, replacing them with self-acceptance and self-love."

11. "I trust in my own inner wisdom and intuition, honoring my own path and decisions."

12. "I choose to see my perceived flaws as opportunities for growth and self-improvement."

13. "I am a work in progress, and I accept myself at every stage of my journey."

14. "I am worthy of forgiveness, and I forgive myself for any past mistakes or shortcomings."

15. "I embrace my authentic self and allow it to shine brightly in the world."

16. "I release the need to be perfect and instead focus on progress and self-acceptance."

17. "I choose to nourish my mind, body, and spirit with love, acceptance, and self-care."

18. "I recognize that self-acceptance is a journey, and I am committed to embracing it every day."

19. "I let go of the need to please others and instead prioritize my own happiness and well-being."

20. "I am at peace with myself, knowing that I am worthy of love, acceptance, and self-compassion."

Repeat these affirmations regularly to cultivate a deep sense of self-acceptance. Embrace your uniqueness, honor your journey, and shower yourself with love, kindness, and understanding. By embracing self-acceptance, you create a foundation of confidence, inner peace, and authenticity that positively impacts your experience as a mother and every aspect of your life.

Affirmations for self-love and body positivity

1. "I love and accept my body exactly as it is, appreciating its strength and uniqueness."

2. "I choose to celebrate my body and treat it with kindness and respect."

3. "I am deserving of love and compassion, including self-love and self-compassion."

4. "I release any negative thoughts or judgments about my body and replace them with love and acceptance."

5. "I am beautiful and worthy, regardless of society's standards or expectations."

6. "I embrace my body with gratitude for all that it allows me to do and experience."

7. "I let go of comparisons and honor the beauty of diversity in body shapes, sizes, and appearances."

8. "I nourish my body with wholesome foods, exercise, and self-care, because I deserve to feel good."

9. "I appreciate and love every part of my body, recognizing that each part serves a unique purpose."

10. "I radiate confidence and self-assurance, knowing that my worth goes beyond physical appearance."

11. "I reject societal pressures and embrace my own definition of beauty and self-worth."

12. "I choose to focus on the positive qualities of my body and nurture a healthy body image."

13. "I am more than my physical appearance. My worth comes from within."

14. "I practice self-care and prioritize activities that make me feel good and enhance my well-being."

15. "I release the need for external validation and find validation within myself, knowing that I am enough."

16. "I speak to myself with kindness and love, replacing self-criticism with self-encouragement."

17. "I am proud of who I am, including my body, and I celebrate my uniqueness."

18. "I embrace my imperfections as a testament to my humanity and beauty."

19. "I am the only one who gets to define my worth and beauty, and I choose to define them positively."

20. "I am grateful for my body and all that it does for me. I choose to love and care for it unconditionally."

Repeat these affirmations daily, allowing them to reinforce self-love and body positivity. Embrace your body as it is, practice self-care, and choose to love and appreciate yourself exactly as you are. By cultivating self-love and body positivity, you empower yourself to live a joyful and confident life, setting an example of self-acceptance for yourself and others.

Affirmations for appreciating the journey of motherhood

1. "I embrace the journey of motherhood with gratitude and joy."

2. "I am grateful for the opportunity to experience the profound love and connection that comes with being a mother."

3. "I cherish the moments, big and small, that make up the beautiful tapestry of motherhood."

4. "I appreciate the growth and personal development that motherhood brings into my life."

5. "I am in awe of the resilience, strength, and patience that I possess as a mother."

6. "I celebrate the milestones and accomplishments of my children, knowing that I am guiding them on their own unique paths."

7. "I find beauty in the chaos and embrace the unpredictability that comes with being a mother."

8. "I recognize that every challenge I face as a mother is an opportunity for personal and emotional growth."

9. "I am proud of the love and care I provide for my children, knowing that I am making a positive impact on their lives."

10. "I trust my instincts as a mother and make decisions with love, compassion, and wisdom."

11. "I find joy in the simple moments of motherhood, savoring the laughter, hugs, and tender moments shared with my children."

12. "I appreciate the lessons I learn from my children, as they remind me of the importance of presence, curiosity, and unconditional love."

13. "I am grateful for the support system I have as a mother, including my partner, family, and friends who share in this journey with me."

14. "I embrace the messiness and imperfections of motherhood, knowing that they are part of the growth and learning process."

15. "I honor and nurture myself as a mother, recognizing that self-care is essential for my well-being and the well-being of my family."

16. "I am present and fully engaged in each moment with my children, creating lasting memories and connections."

17. "I acknowledge that motherhood is a journey of self-discovery and transformation, and I am open to the lessons it teaches me."

18. "I find strength in the challenges I face as a mother, knowing that they shape me into a more compassionate and resilient person."

19. "I appreciate the support and guidance I receive as a mother, and I am grateful for the resources and community that uplift and inspire me."

20. "I celebrate the gift of motherhood and the unconditional love that flows through me and into the lives of my children."

Repeat these affirmations regularly to cultivate a deep appreciation for the journey of motherhood. Embrace the joys, challenges, growth, and love that come with being a mother. By fostering gratitude and presence, you can create a meaningful and fulfilling experience for yourself and your children, cherishing the precious moments along the way.

Affirmations for finding joy in the present moment

1. "I find joy and happiness in the simple moments of life."

2. "I embrace the present moment with open arms, allowing joy to fill my heart."

3. "I choose to let go of worries about the past or future and fully immerse myself in the beauty of the present."

4. "I am grateful for the small pleasures that bring me joy and light up my day."

5. "I find joy in the present moment, knowing that it is the only moment I truly have."

6. "I release expectations and allow myself to be fully present, opening myself up to the joy that surrounds me."

7. "I appreciate the beauty in the ordinary, finding joy in the everyday moments of life."

8. "I cultivate a positive mindset, focusing on the blessings and opportunities that each present moment holds."

9. "I choose to see the world through the lens of joy and find happiness in even the smallest of things."

10. "I celebrate the present moment as a gift, embracing it with gratitude and joy."

11. "I find joy in connecting with others and nurturing meaningful relationships in the present moment."

12. "I let go of distractions and choose to be fully present, allowing myself to experience joy in its purest form."

13. "I find joy in the journey, appreciating the process of growth and self-discovery in each present moment."

14. "I savor the present moment, knowing that it is a precious and irreplaceable part of my life."

15. "I find joy in the beauty of nature, immersing myself in its wonders and finding peace in the present moment."

16. "I embrace the power of mindfulness, anchoring myself in the present and finding joy in the here and now."

17. "I release the need to rush through life and instead choose to slow down and savor the present moment."

18. "I find joy in practicing gratitude, recognizing the abundance that exists in every present moment."

19. "I choose to let go of regrets and focus on the opportunities for joy and happiness that exist in the present moment."

20. "I am fully present in each moment, opening myself up to the infinite possibilities of joy and love."

Repeat these affirmations to remind yourself to find joy in the present moment. Embrace the beauty and blessings that surround you, savoring each experience and finding happiness in the here and now. By cultivating a mindset of presence and gratitude, you can create a more joyful and fulfilling life as a mom and appreciate the precious moments that unfold along your journey.

Nurturing Relationships

A. **The importance of nurturing relationships**

    1.Recognizing the impact of healthy and supportive relationships on well-being

    2. Understanding the role of relationships in fostering emotional connection and fulfillment

    3. Embracing the value of investing time and effort into nurturing relationships

B. Cultivating self-awareness in relationships

    1. Developing an understanding of personal needs, boundaries, and communication styles

    2. Reflecting on past experiences to identify patterns and areas for growth

    3. Practicing active listening and empathy to deepen connections with others

C. Building strong connections with your partner

    1. Prioritizing open and honest communication

    2. Nurturing intimacy and emotional connection

    3. Supporting each other's growth and fostering a sense of partnership

D. Nurturing relationships with family members

    1. Creating meaningful traditions and shared experiences

2. Practicing forgiveness and fostering understanding

3. Cultivating a supportive and loving environment for family members to thrive

E. Fostering friendships and social connections

1. Investing time and energy in nurturing friendships

2. Supporting friends through both joyful and challenging times

3. Cultivating a diverse and supportive social network

F. Nurturing relationships with children

1. Practicing active and attentive parenting

2. Creating a safe and loving environment for children to express themselves

3. Balancing nurturing with fostering independence and growth

G. Embracing self-care within relationships

1. Prioritizing personal well-being and self-care routines

2. Communicating needs and setting boundaries within relationships

3. Recognizing that self-care is essential for nurturing healthy and fulfilling relationships

H. Affirmations for nurturing relationships

1. Affirmations for open and honest communication

2. Affirmations for fostering empathy and understanding

3. Affirmations for building strong and nurturing connections

This chapter focuses on the significance of nurturing relationships in various aspects of life. By cultivating self-awareness, fostering open communication, and practicing empathy, you can create strong and fulfilling connections with your partner, family members, friends, and children. Additionally, recognizing the importance of self-care within relationships allows you to nurture healthy and balanced connections. Repeat the affirmations provided to reinforce positive beliefs and behaviors that support the growth and nurturing of your relationships.

Maintaining healthy relationships amidst motherhood

1. "I prioritize nurturing and maintaining healthy relationships alongside my responsibilities as a mother."

2. "I create space and time for meaningful connections with my loved ones, valuing the importance of these relationships."

3. "I communicate openly and honestly with my loved ones, fostering understanding and trust in our relationships."

4. "I actively listen to the needs and concerns of my loved ones, ensuring their voices are heard and respected."

5. "I set boundaries to maintain a healthy balance between my role as a mother and my relationships with others."

6. "I express gratitude and appreciation for the support and love I receive from my loved ones."

7. "I make time for quality moments with my loved ones, engaging in activities that strengthen our bond."

8. "I prioritize self-care to ensure I have the energy and emotional capacity to invest in my relationships."

9. "I seek support when needed, recognizing that asking for help strengthens my relationships."

10. "I embrace vulnerability and share my joys and challenges with my loved ones, fostering deeper connections."

11. "I find creative ways to stay connected with my loved ones, even when time or distance is a challenge."

12. "I express love and affection to my loved ones, nurturing a warm and loving environment within our relationships."

13. "I actively work on resolving conflicts and disagreements with my loved ones, fostering healthier and stronger bonds."

14. "I create a safe space for open and non-judgmental communication within my relationships."

15. "I prioritize quality time with my loved ones, cherishing the moments we share together."

16. "I balance the needs of my children and the needs of my relationships, ensuring everyone feels valued and supported."

17. "I make conscious efforts to celebrate and honor the individuality of my loved ones, respecting their unique needs and interests."

18. "I cultivate patience and understanding in my relationships, recognizing that motherhood can bring new challenges and adjustments."

19. "I practice forgiveness and let go of grudges, allowing love and compassion to prevail in my relationships."

20. "I embrace the journey of motherhood without losing sight of the importance of maintaining healthy and fulfilling relationships with my loved ones."

Repeat these affirmations regularly to reinforce the commitment to maintaining healthy relationships amidst motherhood. By nurturing and investing in your relationships, you create a strong support system and cultivate fulfilling connections that bring joy, love, and understanding into your life as a mother.

Affirmations for enhancing communication and connection

Affirmations for strengthening romantic relationships

1. "I am committed to nurturing and growing my romantic relationship with love and care."

2. "I communicate openly and honestly with my partner, fostering a deep connection and understanding."

3. "I prioritize quality time with my partner, creating opportunities for bonding and creating cherished memories."

4. "I express love and affection to my partner consistently, nurturing a strong and intimate connection."

5. "I actively listen to my partner's needs and concerns, making them feel valued and heard in our relationship."

6. "I appreciate and celebrate the unique qualities and strengths of my partner, nurturing a sense of admiration and respect."

7. "I prioritize the emotional and physical intimacy in my relationship, fostering a deep and fulfilling connection."

8. "I practice forgiveness and let go of past resentments, creating space for growth and harmony in our relationship."

9. "I show gratitude for my partner's presence and contributions, fostering a positive and appreciative atmosphere in our relationship."

10. "I prioritize regular and open communication with my partner, creating a safe space for vulnerability and understanding."

11. "I support my partner's dreams and goals, encouraging their personal growth and celebrating their achievements."

12. "I seek opportunities for shared interests and experiences, fostering a sense of adventure and excitement in our relationship."

13. "I prioritize romance and nurturing the spark in my relationship, keeping the passion alive and growing stronger."

14. "I respect my partner's boundaries and honor their individuality, fostering a sense of autonomy and trust in our relationship."

15. "I invest time and effort into cultivating trust and deepening the emotional connection with my partner."

16. "I take responsibility for my own actions and communicate openly about any challenges or concerns in our relationship."

17. "I am committed to creating a partnership built on mutual respect, love, and growth."

18. "I seek to understand and support my partner's needs, fostering a strong sense of teamwork and collaboration."

19. "I embrace vulnerability and share my authentic self with my partner, creating an atmosphere of honesty and intimacy."

20. "I am grateful for the love and joy my partner brings into my life, and I continuously work to strengthen and nourish our relationship."

Repeat these affirmations regularly to reinforce the love, commitment, and effort you put into your romantic relationship. By focusing on open communication, understanding, appreciation, and intimacy, you can create a strong and fulfilling partnership that continues to grow and thrive.

Affirmations for fostering friendships and support networks

1. "I attract and cultivate genuine and uplifting friendships in my life."

2. "I am a loyal and supportive friend, offering my love, understanding, and encouragement unconditionally."

3. "I create space for meaningful connections to enter my life, knowing that strong friendships enrich and nourish my well-being."

4. "I celebrate and appreciate the unique qualities and strengths of my friends, fostering a sense of camaraderie and acceptance."

5. "I actively listen to my friends, showing genuine interest in their lives, dreams, and challenges."

6. "I nurture my friendships with regular communication, quality time, and acts of kindness, strengthening the bond we share."

7. "I am a trusted confidant and provide a safe space for my friends to express their

thoughts and feelings without judgment."

8. "I show gratitude for the support and companionship of my friends, expressing my appreciation for their presence in my life."

9. "I am reliable and dependable, offering my support and assistance when my friends are in need."

10. "I celebrate my friends' successes and milestones, rejoicing in their happiness and achievements."

11. "I embrace diversity and cherish the unique perspectives and experiences that my friends bring into my life."

12. "I let go of any past misunderstandings or conflicts and approach my friendships with forgiveness, understanding, and open-heartedness."

13. "I take the initiative to plan and organize social activities, creating opportunities for shared experiences and lasting memories."

14. "I am a source of positivity, encouragement, and inspiration for my friends, uplifting and motivating them on their journey."

15. "I respect the boundaries, individuality, and autonomy of my friends, allowing them the freedom to be their authentic selves."

16. "I attract friends who align with my values, support my personal growth, and contribute positively to my well-being."

17. "I actively seek to expand my support network, fostering connections with like-minded individuals who uplift and inspire me."

18. "I prioritize selflessness and empathy, offering a listening ear, a helping hand, and emotional support to my friends."

19. "I am a beacon of kindness, compassion, and understanding, creating an environment of trust and safety within my friendships."

20. "I am grateful for the beautiful friendships in my life and continue to invest time,

love, and energy in nurturing and deepening these connections."

Repeat these affirmations regularly to reinforce your commitment to fostering friendships and support networks. By embodying qualities of kindness, understanding, and gratitude, you attract and cultivate meaningful connections that bring joy, support, and a sense of belonging into your life.

Affirmations for nurturing relationships with children

1. "I am a loving and nurturing parent, providing a safe and supportive environment for my children to grow and thrive."

2. "I cherish and appreciate the unique qualities and strengths of each of my children, fostering their individuality and self-esteem."

3. "I am present and engaged with my children, actively listening to their thoughts, feelings, and experiences."

4. "I create a loving and open-hearted connection with my children, fostering a deep sense of trust and emotional intimacy."

5. "I prioritize quality time with my children, engaging in activities that strengthen our bond and create lasting memories."

6. "I provide consistent and clear communication, setting loving boundaries that support their growth and well-being."

7. "I practice patience and understanding, meeting my children where they are in their development and offering guidance with love and compassion."

8. "I celebrate my children's achievements and successes, recognizing and acknowledging their efforts and strengths."

9. "I actively support and encourage my children's dreams and passions, nurturing their sense of curiosity and self-discovery."

10. "I am a role model of kindness, empathy, and respect, teaching my children valuable life lessons through my words and actions."

11. "I express my love and affection for my children regularly, letting them know they are cherished and valued."

12. "I create a nurturing and loving home environment that fosters a sense of security, comfort, and belonging for my children."

13. "I actively listen and validate my children's emotions, providing a safe space for them to express themselves authentically."

14. "I practice forgiveness and understanding, teaching my children the importance of empathy and the power of second chances."

15. "I cultivate curiosity and a love for learning in my children, supporting their educational and personal growth."

16. "I teach and encourage healthy habits, both physically and emotionally, to help my children develop resilience and well-being."

17. "I embrace playfulness and joy in my interactions with my children, nurturing their sense of wonder and imagination."

18. "I provide guidance and discipline with love and understanding, teaching my children valuable life skills and responsibility."

19. "I foster independence and self-confidence in my children, allowing them to explore and make choices while providing a safety net of support."

20. "I am grateful for the privilege of being a parent, and I continuously work on deepening and nurturing the loving relationship I have with my children."

Repeat these affirmations regularly to reinforce the love, care, and commitment you have for nurturing your relationship with your children. By embodying these affirmations, you create a strong foundation of trust, love, and connection that supports their growth, well-being, and happiness.

Empowering Mom's Inner Voice

A. Recognizing the power of self-talk and inner dialogue

1.Understanding the impact of self-talk on self-esteem and confidence

2. Acknowledging the influence of inner dialogue on decision-making and well-being

3. Embracing the importance of empowering and positive self-talk

B. Cultivating self-awareness of negative self-talk patterns

1. Identifying common negative self-talk patterns and their origins

2. Bringing awareness to the impact of negative self-talk on self-image and mental well-being

3. Practicing self-compassion and self-forgiveness in response to negative self-talk

C. Rewriting negative self-talk with empowering affirmations

1. Creating a list of empowering affirmations that challenge and replace negative self-talk

2. Practicing and integrating empowering affirmations into daily self-talk routines

3. Embracing the transformative power of positive self-talk on confidence and self-belief

D. Harnessing the power of affirmations for self-empowerment

1. Understanding the science and psychology behind affirmations

2. Exploring different techniques for incorporating affirmations into daily life

3. Utilizing affirmations to cultivate self-empowerment, resilience, and self-confidence

E. Nurturing self-belief and embracing personal strengths

1. Recognizing and celebrating personal strengths and achievements

2. Challenging self-doubt and fostering a belief in one's own capabilities

3. Embracing a growth mindset and cultivating self-belief in the face of challenges

F. Embracing self-compassion and self-acceptance

1. Practicing self-compassion as a foundation for positive self-talk and inner empowerment

2. Letting go of self-judgment and embracing self-acceptance

3. Cultivating a loving and supportive relationship with oneself

G. Affirmations for empowering mom's inner voice

1. Affirmations for cultivating self-belief and confidence

2. Affirmations for embracing self-compassion and self-acceptance

3. Affirmations for challenging negative self-talk and fostering inner empowerment

This chapter focuses on empowering and nurturing the inner voice of moms. By recognizing and addressing negative self-talk patterns, rewriting them with empowering affirmations, and cultivating self-belief and self-compassion, moms can harness the power of their inner voice to boost confidence, resilience, and well-being. Repeat the provided affirmations to reinforce positive self-talk and cultivate a loving and empowering inner dialogue.

Harnessing the power of positive self-talk

1. "I am my biggest cheerleader, and I fill my mind with positive and empowering thoughts."

2. "I choose to replace self-doubt with self-belief, knowing that I am capable of achieving great things."

3. "I speak to myself with kindness, love, and encouragement, uplifting my spirit and nurturing my confidence."

4. "I celebrate my strengths and accomplishments, acknowledging the value I bring to the world."

5. "I embrace challenges as opportunities for growth and learning, knowing that I have the resilience to overcome them."

6. "I trust in my abilities and make decisions with confidence, knowing that I am capable of making the right choices."

7. "I choose to focus on solutions rather than problems, approaching obstacles with a positive and optimistic mindset."

8. "I am worthy of success and happiness, and I deserve to pursue my dreams with passion and determination."

9. "I let go of self-limiting beliefs and embrace the limitless possibilities that exist within me and in the world."

10. "I am enough just as I am, and I embrace my unique qualities and contributions."

11. "I attract positivity and abundance into my life by aligning my thoughts and words with my desires."

12. "I radiate confidence and authenticity, inspiring others with my positive energy and self-assuredness."

13. "I choose to see failures as stepping stones to success, learning and growing from each experience."

14. "I am deserving of love, respect, and happiness, and I surround myself with people who uplift and support me."

15. "I trust in my intuition and inner wisdom, knowing that I have the answers within me."

16. "I am in control of my thoughts and emotions, and I choose to cultivate a positive and empowering mindset."

17. "I embrace the journey of self-discovery and personal growth, knowing that I am continually evolving and becoming the best version of myself."

18. "I release comparison and embrace my own unique path, appreciating the progress I have made and the potential that lies ahead."

19. "I attract positive experiences and opportunities into my life by maintaining a positive outlook and belief in myself."

20. "I am grateful for all that I am and all that I have, and I approach each day with a mindset of gratitude and positivity."

Repeat these affirmations regularly to harness the power of positive self-talk. By consciously choosing uplifting and empowering thoughts, you shape your inner dialogue and create a foundation of self-belief, confidence, and resilience. Embrace the power of positive self-talk to transform your mindset and experience greater joy, fulfillment, and success in all areas of your life as a mom.

Affirmations for cultivating self-belief and confidence

1. "I believe in myself and my abilities to overcome any challenge that comes my way."

2. "I am confident in my unique talents and gifts, and I use them to make a positive impact in the world."

3. "I trust in my intuition and make decisions with confidence and clarity."

4. "I am deserving of success and I embrace opportunities that come my way."

5. "I am capable and resilient, and I can handle whatever life brings me."

6. "I am confident in expressing my ideas and opinions, knowing that they hold value and worth."

7. "I stand tall in my authenticity and embrace my true self without seeking validation from others."

8. "I radiate self-assurance and attract positive opportunities and experiences into my life."

9. "I let go of self-doubt and step outside of my comfort zone to embrace growth and personal development."

10. "I am proud of my accomplishments and I celebrate my achievements, no matter how big or small."

11. "I have the power to create the life I desire, and I take inspired action towards my goals."

12. "I am deserving of love, respect, and happiness, and I surround myself with people who uplift and support me."

13. "I acknowledge and appreciate my strengths, using them to overcome obstacles and achieve my dreams."

14. "I embrace failure as an opportunity for learning and growth, and I bounce back stronger than before."

15. "I let go of comparison and embrace my own unique journey, recognizing that I am enough just as I am."

16. "I release negative self-talk and replace it with empowering and uplifting thoughts."

17. "I am confident in setting healthy boundaries and prioritizing my own needs and well-being."

18. "I trust in my ability to handle uncertainty and adapt to change with grace and resilience."

19. "I surround myself with positive and supportive influences that encourage my self-belief and confidence."

20. "I am a powerful creator, and I manifest my desires with unwavering belief and confidence."

Repeat these affirmations daily to cultivate self-belief and confidence. By affirming your worth, embracing your strengths, and trusting in your abilities, you build a strong foundation of self-confidence that empowers you to pursue your goals, overcome challenges, and live a fulfilling life. Embrace these affirmations and let them guide you towards greater self-belief and unwavering confidence.

Affirmations for recognizing personal achievements

1. Affirmations for recognizing personal achievements

2. "I acknowledge and celebrate my accomplishments, no matter how big or small."

3. "I am proud of myself for the progress I have made on my journey."

4. "I recognize and appreciate the hard work and effort I have put into reaching my goals."

5. "I celebrate the milestones I have achieved and the growth I have experienced along the way."

6. "I give myself credit for the challenges I have overcome and the obstacles I have conquered."

7. "I take time to reflect on my achievements and feel a sense of pride and satisfaction."

8. "I honor the dedication and commitment I have shown in pursuing my dreams."

9. "I embrace my achievements as stepping stones to even greater success and

fulfillment."

10. "I am grateful for the opportunities I have had to showcase my skills and talents."

11. "I acknowledge the impact of my achievements on myself and others, and I am grateful for the positive influence I have had."

12. "I celebrate my unique journey and the personal growth I have experienced along the way."

13. "I recognize that every step forward is an achievement, and I give myself credit for each milestone reached."

14. "I let go of comparing my achievements to others and focus on my own progress and growth."

15. "I am deserving of recognition and praise for my hard work and dedication."

16. "I appreciate the effort and perseverance it took to accomplish my goals."

17. "I acknowledge the courage it took to step outside of my comfort zone and pursue my dreams."

18. "I am proud of the skills and talents I have developed and the positive impact they have in my life and the lives of others."

19. "I celebrate the lessons I have learned from my failures and mistakes, recognizing that they have contributed to my growth."

20. "I embrace a mindset of continuous improvement and recognize that my achievements are a result of ongoing learning and development."

21. "I celebrate myself for who I am and the progress I have made on my unique path."

Repeat these affirmations regularly to honor and recognize your personal achievements. By acknowledging your accomplishments, you cultivate a sense of pride, gratitude, and self-worth. Embrace and celebrate your journey, for each step forward is a testament to your strength, resilience, and growth.

Affirmations for embracing personal growth

1. Affirmations for embracing personal growth

2. "I embrace personal growth as a lifelong journey of learning and self-discovery."

3. "I am open to new experiences and opportunities that contribute to my personal growth."

4. "I welcome challenges as opportunities for growth and transformation."

5. "I am committed to expanding my knowledge, skills, and abilities."

6. "I embrace change and adaptability, knowing that it leads to personal growth."

7. "I release fear and resistance, allowing myself to step out of my comfort zone and embrace new possibilities."

8. "I celebrate the progress I have made on my personal growth journey."

9. "I am curious and seek out opportunities for self-reflection and self-improvement."

10. "I embrace feedback and constructive criticism as valuable tools for personal

growth."

11. "I trust in my own potential and capacity for personal growth and development."

12. "I let go of limiting beliefs and embrace a growth mindset, knowing that I can continuously learn and improve."

13. "I am patient with myself as I navigate challenges and setbacks, knowing that they contribute to my personal growth."

14. "I celebrate small victories along the way, recognizing that personal growth is a series of steps and progress."

15. "I am committed to my own self-care and well-being, nurturing my physical, mental, and emotional health."

16. "I surround myself with supportive and growth-oriented individuals who inspire and challenge me to be the best version of myself."

17. "I embrace self-reflection and self-awareness, understanding that it is key to personal growth."

18. "I am resilient and bounce back stronger from setbacks, using them as opportunities for learning and growth."

19. "I let go of comparison and focus on my own personal growth journey, recognizing that everyone's path is unique."

20. "I celebrate my personal growth milestones and acknowledge the positive changes I have made in my life."

21. "I am constantly evolving and becoming the best version of myself through ongoing personal growth and self-improvement."

Repeat these affirmations regularly to embrace personal growth and development. By cultivating a mindset of openness, curiosity, and self-reflection, you create a fertile ground for continuous learning and improvement. Embrace the transformative power of personal growth and celebrate the progress you make along your journey.

Affirmations for stepping into one's own power

1. "I am powerful, capable, and worthy of all the success and happiness that comes my way."

2. "I embrace my unique strengths and talents, using them to create positive change in my life and the lives of others."

3. "I confidently express my needs, desires, and boundaries, knowing that my voice matters."

4. "I release self-doubt and step into my power with courage and conviction."

5. "I trust in my intuition and make decisions with confidence, knowing that I have the wisdom within me."

6. "I am the author of my own life story, and I take full responsibility for creating the life I desire."

7. "I let go of the need for external validation and approval, knowing that my worthiness comes from within."

8. "I stand tall in my authenticity and shine my light brightly for the world to see."

9. "I use my power and influence to uplift and inspire others, making a positive impact in the world."

10. "I embrace challenges as opportunities to grow and prove my resilience and strength."

11. "I am not limited by my past or present circumstances; I have the power to create a brighter future."

12. "I release the fear of failure and embrace the mindset of growth and possibility."

13. "I attract abundance and success into my life by aligning my thoughts and actions with my highest potential."

14. "I surround myself with supportive and empowering individuals who believe in my abilities and dreams."

15. "I celebrate my achievements and milestones, acknowledging the progress I have made on my journey."

16. "I let go of comparison and embrace my own unique path, knowing that my journey is worthy and significant."

17. "I am deserving of success, happiness, and fulfillment, and I claim it with confidence and gratitude."

18. "I trust in my abilities to overcome obstacles and navigate challenges with grace and resilience."

19. "I use my power responsibly and consciously, always considering the well-being of myself and others."

20. "I step into my power with love and compassion, recognizing that true power comes from a place of authenticity and kindness."

Repeat these affirmations regularly to step into your own power and embrace your inherent potential. By affirming your worthiness, capabilities, and personal power, you empower yourself to create the life you desire and make a positive impact in the world.

Embrace and embody your inner power, and let it guide you towards a life of purpose, fulfillment, and joy.

Practicing Gratitude

A. **Understanding the transformative power of gratitude**

1.Exploring the scientific benefits of practicing gratitude

2. Recognizing how gratitude shifts perspective and enhances well-being

3. Embracing gratitude as a daily practice for cultivating happiness and contentment

B. Cultivating a gratitude mindset

1. Developing awareness of the present moment and the blessings within it

2. Shifting focus from scarcity to abundance by acknowledging blessings in life

3. Practicing mindfulness to deepen gratitude and appreciation for the present

C. Gratitude practices and rituals

1. Keeping a gratitude journal to document daily blessings and positive experiences

2. Expressing gratitude to others through heartfelt gestures, notes, or acts of kindness

3. Creating gratitude rituals, such as gratitude walks or meditation, to anchor the practice into daily life

D. Finding gratitude in challenging times

1. Cultivating resilience and finding silver linings in difficult situations

2. Shifting perspective to recognize the lessons and growth opportunities in challenges

3. Using gratitude as a tool for self-care and emotional well-being during tough times

E. Gratitude for self-care and well-being
1. Practicing self-compassion and gratitude for oneself

2. Appreciating the body, mind, and spirit as sources of well-being and vitality

3. Integrating gratitude into self-care routines to foster a positive and nurturing relationship with oneself

F. Gratitude in relationships and parenting
1. Expressing gratitude to loved ones and acknowledging their contributions

2. Teaching and modeling gratitude to children to cultivate appreciation and kindness

3. Strengthening bonds through shared gratitude practices and acts of gratitude within relationships

G. Gratitude for the journey of motherhood
1. Finding gratitude in the joys and challenges of motherhood

2. Appreciating the growth and transformation that comes with being a mother

3. Cultivating gratitude for the love, connection, and cherished moments experienced as a mother

H. Affirmations for practicing gratitude
1. Affirmations for cultivating a grateful mindset

2. Affirmations for finding gratitude in challenging times

3. Affirmations for expressing gratitude and appreciation in relationships

This chapter explores the transformative power of gratitude and provides practical strategies for cultivating a grateful mindset. By practicing gratitude daily, embracing challenges with gratitude, and fostering gratitude in relationships and motherhood, moms can experience increased happiness, contentment, and overall well-being. Incorporate these affirmations into your gratitude practice to deepen your appreciation for life's blessings and cultivate a mindset of gratitude and abundance.

The transformative effects of gratitude

1. Gratitude shifts your focus from scarcity to abundance, allowing you to appreciate the blessings in your life.

2. Practicing gratitude enhances your overall well-being and promotes a positive mindset.

3. Gratitude cultivates a sense of contentment and fulfillment, helping you find joy in the present moment.

4. It reduces stress and anxiety, promoting greater emotional resilience and mental well-being.

5. Gratitude strengthens relationships by fostering appreciation and deepening connections with others.

6. It improves physical health by reducing symptoms of stress and promoting self-care behaviors.

7. Gratitude increases self-esteem and self-worth, allowing you to recognize your own value and strengths.

8. It enhances empathy and compassion, leading to more harmonious and supportive interactions with others.

9. Gratitude helps you navigate and find meaning in difficult times, providing a perspective of growth and resilience.

10. It fosters a positive outlook and optimistic mindset, empowering you to overcome challenges and embrace opportunities.

11. Gratitude improves sleep quality and promotes relaxation, leading to better overall health and well-being.

12. It boosts your overall happiness and life satisfaction, bringing a greater sense of fulfillment and purpose.

13. Gratitude strengthens your ability to appreciate the simple joys and beauty in everyday life.

14. It encourages a mindset of abundance, attracting more positive experiences and opportunities into your life.

15. Gratitude promotes mindfulness and presence, allowing you to fully engage and savor the present moment.

16. It fosters a sense of interconnectedness and appreciation for the world around you.

17. Gratitude cultivates resilience and helps you bounce back from setbacks with grace and gratitude.

18. It inspires acts of kindness and generosity, creating a ripple effect of positivity and goodwill.

19. Gratitude increases your overall energy and vitality, promoting a sense of vitality and aliveness.

20. It provides a powerful tool for personal growth and self-reflection, allowing you to continuously evolve and become the best version of yourself.

Embrace the transformative effects of gratitude by incorporating gratitude practices into your daily life. By nurturing a grateful mindset, you can experience profound positive changes in your overall well-being, relationships, and outlook on life.

Affirmations for cultivating a grateful mindset

1. "I am grateful for the abundance of blessings in my life, both big and small."

2. "I choose to focus on the positive aspects of my life and express gratitude for them."

3. "I appreciate the simple joys and beauty that surround me each day."

4. "I am thankful for the love and support I receive from family and friends."

5. "I find gratitude in every experience, knowing that each holds valuable lessons for my growth."

6. "I express gratitude for the opportunities that come my way, embracing them with open arms."

7. "I am deeply grateful for my health and well-being, nurturing and caring for my body, mind, and spirit."

8. "I recognize the abundance in my life and let gratitude fill my heart and soul."

9. "I choose to see challenges as opportunities for growth and transformation,

finding gratitude in the lessons they offer."

10. "I appreciate the beauty of nature and the wonders of the world around me."

11. "I am grateful for the lessons learned from past experiences, as they have shaped me into who I am today."

12. "I express gratitude for the moments of joy, laughter, and love that enrich my life."

13. "I am thankful for the opportunities that allow me to pursue my passions and live a fulfilling life."

14. "I am grateful for the support and encouragement I receive on my journey, knowing that I am not alone."

15. "I appreciate the little acts of kindness and the positive impact they have on my life."

16. "I express gratitude for the gift of each new day, embracing it with a grateful and open heart."

17. "I am grateful for the strength and resilience within me, knowing that I can overcome any challenge."

18. "I find gratitude in the relationships I have, cherishing the connections and love shared with others."

19. "I express gratitude for the moments of peace and stillness that bring calmness to my soul."

20. "I am grateful for the opportunity to give back and make a positive difference in the lives of others."

Repeat these affirmations daily to cultivate a grateful mindset. Allow gratitude to become a natural part of your thoughts and actions, and let it transform your perspective, bringing joy, contentment, and a deeper appreciation for the blessings in your life. Embrace the power of gratitude and watch as it enhances your well-being and brings greater fulfillment to your daily experiences.

Affirmations for finding gratitude in everyday moments

1. "I find gratitude in the simple pleasures and small moments that bring me joy."

2. "I appreciate the beauty of each new day, finding gratitude in the opportunity it brings."

3. "I am grateful for the warmth of the sun on my skin and the gentle breeze that refreshes me."

4. "I find gratitude in the delicious taste of food that nourishes and satisfies me."

5. "I appreciate the cozy moments of relaxation and the comfort of my surroundings."

6. "I am grateful for the laughter and smiles shared with loved ones, creating cherished memories."

7. "I find gratitude in the kindness of strangers, recognizing the positive impact they have on my day."

8. "I appreciate the peace and stillness that allows me to reconnect with myself and

find inner calm."

9. "I am grateful for the lessons learned from challenges, knowing they contribute to my growth and resilience."

10. "I find gratitude in the beauty of nature, observing its wonders and feeling a sense of awe."

11. "I appreciate the soothing sounds of music and the way it uplifts and touches my soul."

12. "I am grateful for the opportunity to learn and expand my knowledge, embracing the gift of curiosity."

13. "I find gratitude in the moments of solitude that allow me to reflect and reconnect with my inner self."

14. "I appreciate the comfort and love of my home, creating a safe haven for relaxation and rejuvenation."

15. "I am grateful for the technology that connects me with loved ones and opens doors to new experiences."

16. "I find gratitude in the beauty of art and creativity, inspiring me to express myself authentically."

17. "I appreciate the joy of learning something new, expanding my horizons and embracing personal growth."

18. "I am grateful for the feeling of accomplishment and satisfaction that comes from completing tasks and goals."

19. "I find gratitude in the moments of laughter and playfulness, bringing lightness and happiness into my day."

20. "I appreciate the love and companionship of my pets, bringing warmth and joy to my life."

Repeat these affirmations regularly to shift your focus to the everyday moments that hold beauty, joy, and gratitude. By cultivating gratitude for the small blessings in your life, you will find a deeper sense of appreciation and contentment, enhancing your overall well-being and happiness. Embrace the present moment and allow gratitude to illuminate your everyday experiences.

Affirmations for appreciating the blessings of motherhood

1. "I am grateful for the miracle of motherhood and the precious gift of my children."

2. "I appreciate the love and joy that fills my heart as I witness my children grow and thrive."

3. "I am grateful for the unique bond I share with each of my children, cherishing the moments we spend together."

4. "I appreciate the laughter and playfulness that fills our home, creating a warm and loving environment."

5. "I am grateful for the lessons I learn from my children, as they constantly remind me of the beauty of innocence and curiosity."

6. "I appreciate the unconditional love I receive from my children, knowing that it is a precious and priceless gift."

7. "I am grateful for the opportunity to guide and nurture my children, watching them blossom into their true selves."

8. "I appreciate the role of being a mother, recognizing the profound impact it has on shaping the future generation."

9. "I am grateful for the challenges I face as a mother, as they provide opportunities for growth and self-discovery."

10. "I appreciate the moments of connection and bonding with my children, creating lifelong memories and deepening our relationship."

11. "I am grateful for the support and understanding I receive from other mothers, knowing that we are all on this journey together."

12. "I appreciate the selflessness and sacrifices that come with motherhood, as they reflect the depth of my love for my children."

13. "I am grateful for the daily reminders of gratitude that motherhood brings, as it teaches me to appreciate the little things in life."

14. "I appreciate the laughter and silliness that my children bring into my life, bringing lightness and joy to each day."

15. "I am grateful for the opportunity to witness the growth and development of my children, feeling a sense of pride and fulfillment."

16. "I appreciate the support and encouragement I receive as a mother, knowing that I am not alone in this journey."

17. "I am grateful for the love and guidance I provide to my children, knowing that it shapes their lives in profound ways."

18. "I appreciate the moments of stillness and reflection that motherhood brings, allowing me to appreciate the beauty of the present."

19. "I am grateful for the special bond I share with my children, cherishing the unbreakable connection we have."

20. "I appreciate the transformative power of motherhood, as it allows me to grow, learn, and evolve into the best version of myself."

Repeat these affirmations regularly to deepen your appreciation for the blessings of motherhood. Embrace the unique experiences and joys that come with being a mother, and allow gratitude to fill your heart as you navigate this beautiful journey. Celebrate the love, growth, and connection that motherhood brings, and let gratitude guide you as you create cherished memories with your children.

Affirmations for fostering an attitude of abundance

1. "I am grateful for the abundance of opportunities that surround me each day."

2. "I embrace the abundance of love, joy, and blessings that flow into my life."

3. "I attract abundance in all areas of my life, knowing that I am deserving of prosperity."

4. "I am open to receiving abundance in its various forms, allowing it to manifest in my life."

5. "I appreciate the abundance of resources and support available to me as I pursue my dreams."

6. "I am grateful for the abundance of time and energy I have to devote to my passions and goals."

7. "I celebrate the abundance of creativity and inspiration that flows through me, fueling my endeavors."

8. "I am grateful for the abundance of opportunities for personal and professional growth that come my way."

9. "I embrace an attitude of gratitude, knowing that it attracts even more abundance into my life."

10. "I am abundant in love, kindness, and compassion, sharing these qualities with others."

11. "I appreciate the abundance of beauty in the world, finding joy in the simple wonders of life."

12. "I am grateful for the abundance of connections and relationships that enrich my life."

13. "I embrace the abundance of knowledge and wisdom available to me, continuously learning and growing."

14. "I am open to receiving the financial abundance that allows me to live a fulfilling and abundant life."

15. "I appreciate the abundance of health and vitality that supports my well-being and enables me to thrive."

16. "I am grateful for the abundance of opportunities to make a positive impact in the lives of others."

17. "I embrace the abundance mindset, releasing scarcity and embracing the infinite possibilities that surround me."

18. "I am abundant in gratitude, recognizing and celebrating the abundance that already exists in my life."

19. "I appreciate the abundance of peace and serenity that fills my heart and brings balance to my life."

20. "I am grateful for the abundance of experiences and adventures that enrich my journey."

Repeat these affirmations daily to foster an attitude of abundance. By embracing a mindset of abundance, you shift your focus to the richness and prosperity that already exist in your life. Allow gratitude to open your eyes to the countless blessings and opportunities that surround you, and watch as abundance flows into every aspect of your life. Embrace the abundance mindset and live a life filled with gratitude, abundance, and fulfillment.

Embracing Mindfulness

A. **Understanding the concept of mindfulness**

    1.Exploring the meaning and benefits of mindfulness in daily life

    2. Recognizing the power of being present and fully engaged in the present moment

    3. Embracing mindfulness as a tool for reducing stress, enhancing well-being, and cultivating inner peace

B. Cultivating mindfulness in everyday activities

    1. Practicing mindful breathing to anchor yourself in the present moment

    2. Engaging in mindful eating to savor the flavors and textures of food

    3. Incorporating mindfulness into daily routines such as showering, walking, and driving

C. Developing a mindfulness meditation practice

    1. Exploring different meditation techniques and finding what resonates with you

    2. Creating a dedicated space and time for meditation practice

    3. Cultivating a non-judgmental and compassionate attitude towards your thoughts and experiences during meditation

D. Applying mindfulness to stress management and emotional well-being

1. Using mindfulness to observe and manage stress triggers and reactions

2. Cultivating self-compassion and self-care through mindful awareness of your emotions and needs

3. Practicing mindfulness-based stress reduction techniques to promote resilience and emotional balance

E. Enhancing relationships through mindful communication

1. Applying mindful listening and presence in conversations with loved ones

2. Cultivating empathy and understanding through mindful communication

3. Using mindfulness to navigate conflicts and cultivate harmonious relationships

F. Mindfulness in parenting and motherhood

1. Bringing mindful awareness to interactions with children, fostering deeper connection and understanding

2. Using mindfulness to navigate the challenges and stressors of motherhood with greater ease and presence

3. Cultivating self-compassion and mindfulness in self-care as a mother

G. Mindfulness for self-discovery and personal growth

1. Using mindfulness to explore your inner thoughts, beliefs, and desires

2. Cultivating self-awareness and self-acceptance through mindful introspection

3. Embracing mindfulness as a path for personal transformation and growth

H. Affirmations for embracing mindfulness

1. Affirmations for anchoring in the present moment and cultivating awareness

2. Affirmations for finding peace and calm amidst daily challenges

3. Affirmations for integrating mindfulness into daily life as a mom

In this chapter, explore the practice of mindfulness and its profound impact on your well-being as a mom. Learn how to cultivate mindfulness in everyday activities, develop a meditation practice, and apply mindfulness to stress management, relationships, parenting, and personal growth. Embrace the power of mindfulness to enhance your presence, reduce stress, and cultivate inner peace as you navigate the beautiful journey of motherhood. Use the provided affirmations to anchor yourself in the present moment and infuse mindfulness into your daily life.

Understanding the benefits of mindfulness for moms

1. Reduced stress and anxiety: Mindfulness practices help moms manage stress and reduce anxiety by promoting relaxation and fostering a sense of calmness and centeredness.

2. Improved emotional well-being: Mindfulness allows moms to develop a greater awareness of their emotions, helping them respond to challenging situations with more clarity, compassion, and emotional balance.

3. Enhanced focus and concentration: Mindfulness practices help moms improve their focus and concentration, enabling them to be more present and attentive to their children, work, and daily tasks.

4. Increased self-care and self-compassion: Mindfulness encourages moms to prioritize self-care and self-compassion, allowing them to nurture their own well-being and recharge their physical, mental, and emotional energy.

5. Better decision-making: By cultivating mindfulness, moms develop the ability to make thoughtful and conscious decisions, considering the needs and values of themselves and their families.

6. Improved patience and resilience: Mindfulness practices equip moms with tools to cultivate patience and resilience, helping them navigate the ups and downs of motherhood with greater equanimity and adaptability.

7. Strengthened relationships: Mindfulness enhances moms' ability to be fully present and attentive in their interactions with their children, partners, and loved ones, fostering deeper connections and more meaningful relationships.

8. Enhanced self-awareness: Mindfulness practices increase moms' self-awareness, allowing them to understand their thoughts, emotions, and behaviors more deeply, leading to personal growth and self-discovery.

9. Increased gratitude and appreciation: Mindfulness encourages moms to cultivate gratitude and appreciation for the precious moments and blessings in their lives, fostering a sense of contentment and joy.

10. Better stress management: Mindfulness equips moms with effective stress management tools, helping them regulate their emotions, handle challenging situations with greater resilience, and maintain overall well-being.

By embracing mindfulness, moms can experience these profound benefits, enhancing their overall quality of life, well-being, and fulfillment in their role as mothers.

Affirmations for being present and mindful

1. "I am fully present in this moment, embracing the beauty and joy it holds."

2. "I release thoughts of the past and worries about the future, grounding myself in the present moment."

3. "I cultivate a mindful presence, savoring each experience with all my senses."

4. "I bring my full attention to the present, allowing it to unfold with curiosity and openness."

5. "I embrace the power of now, knowing that this moment is where life truly happens."

6. "I let go of distractions and bring my focus to the present moment, immersing myself fully in what I am doing."

7. "I practice mindfulness in my daily activities, finding peace and tranquility in the simplest tasks."

8. "I choose to slow down and savor each moment, honoring the sacredness of the present."

9. "I cultivate awareness and mindfulness, tuning into the needs of my body, mind, and spirit."

10. "I release judgment and embrace acceptance, allowing each moment to be as it is without resistance."

11. "I bring mindfulness to my interactions with others, listening with full presence and offering my authentic self."

12. "I am mindful of my thoughts, choosing thoughts that support my well-being and positivity."

13. "I nurture a sense of gratitude and appreciation for the present moment, finding joy in the simple pleasures."

14. "I practice self-compassion and kindness, extending the same mindfulness and love to myself as I do to others."

15. "I anchor myself in the present moment through mindful breathing, allowing it to bring me calmness and clarity."

16. "I find balance and peace in the present moment, embracing the ebb and flow of life with grace and mindfulness."

17. "I release the need for control and surrender to the flow of the present moment, trusting in its wisdom."

18. "I bring mindfulness to my parenting, cherishing the precious moments with my children and cultivating deeper connections."

19. "I take time for stillness and silence, allowing mindfulness to nourish my soul and bring me inner peace."

20. "I am a beacon of mindfulness, radiating presence, peace, and love to all those around me."

Repeat these affirmations regularly to cultivate a mindful and present mindset. By affirming your intention to be present and embracing mindfulness, you invite a deeper sense of awareness, peace, and joy into your life as a mom. Embrace the power of the present moment and let it guide you in creating meaningful connections, finding balance, and experiencing the beauty of each passing moment.

Affirmations for grounding and centering oneself

1. "I am grounded and centered in the present moment, rooted like a sturdy tree."

2. "I release any tension or stress, allowing my body and mind to find a state of calm and stability."

3. "I connect with the Earth beneath me, feeling its support and nurturing energy."

4. "I am present and fully anchored in my body, feeling the sensations and grounding energy it provides."

5. "I breathe deeply, allowing each breath to ground me and bring me back to the present moment."

6. "I release any distractions or worries, focusing my attention on the present and finding inner balance."

7. "I am connected to my core essence, feeling a deep sense of inner peace and strength."

8. "I visualize roots growing from my feet, grounding me into the Earth and providing stability."

9. "I release any scattered thoughts or emotions, returning to a centered state of clarity and focus."

10. "I find solace in stillness, allowing myself to be fully present and centered in this moment."

11. "I acknowledge and honor my own needs and boundaries, creating a strong foundation within myself."

12. "I am supported and guided by my inner wisdom, allowing it to lead me on my path."

13. "I let go of external pressures and expectations, centering myself in my own values and truth."

14. "I am a calm and steady force amidst the chaos, finding strength in my grounded presence."

15. "I connect with the present moment through mindfulness, finding peace and serenity within."

16. "I release any attachments to the past or worries about the future, focusing on the power of the present."

17. "I am grounded in my breath, using it as an anchor to bring me back to the present whenever needed."

18. "I trust in my own inner guidance, knowing that I am capable of finding my center in any situation."

19. "I embrace the stillness within me, finding peace and tranquility in the present moment."

20. "I am grounded, centered, and aligned with the universe, embracing my true essence."

Repeat these affirmations whenever you feel the need to ground and center yourself. Allow them to anchor you in the present moment, providing stability, clarity, and a sense of inner peace. By grounding and centering yourself, you cultivate a strong foundation from which you can navigate the challenges of motherhood with grace and stability. Embrace your power to find your center and allow it to guide you in living a balanced and fulfilling life.

Affirmations for finding calm amidst chaos

1. "I am the calm amidst the chaos, finding peace within myself regardless of external circumstances."

2. "I breathe in serenity and exhale stress, allowing calmness to flow through me."

3. "I release the need to control and embrace the flow of life, finding inner tranquility amidst chaos."

4. "I remain grounded and centered, bringing a sense of calmness to any situation I encounter."

5. "I trust in my ability to handle challenges with grace and composure, finding calm amidst chaos."

6. "I release resistance and embrace acceptance, finding peace in the present moment, no matter what is happening around me."

7. "I cultivate a peaceful mindset, choosing to respond to chaos with patience, understanding, and love."

8. "I find solace in stillness, allowing it to restore my peace of mind and bring clarity

to chaotic situations."

9. "I tap into my inner resilience and strength, navigating chaos with a calm and steady presence."

10. "I prioritize self-care and create moments of calm amidst chaos, nourishing my well-being and restoring balance."

11. "I release the need to rush and slow down, finding calmness and clarity in the present moment."

12. "I anchor myself in the present, letting go of worries about the future and finding peace in the here and now."

13. "I focus on what I can control and release what is beyond my influence, allowing peace to prevail."

14. "I surround myself with positive energy and cultivate a peaceful environment, supporting calmness amidst chaos."

15. "I am in control of my emotions, choosing peace and calmness as my response to chaos."

16. "I practice deep breathing and mindfulness, using them as tools to find tranquility in the midst of chaos."

17. "I trust that I have the resources and capabilities to navigate any chaotic situation with grace and calmness."

18. "I release the need for perfection and embrace the beauty of imperfections, finding peace amidst the chaos of daily life."

19. "I choose to focus on solutions rather than dwelling on the chaos, allowing calmness to guide my actions."

20. "I affirm my inner peace and carry it with me wherever I go, remaining calm and centered amidst any chaos."

Repeat these affirmations as a reminder of your ability to find calmness and tranquility within yourself, even in the midst of chaos. By affirming your inner peace and choosing calmness as your response to chaotic situations, you empower yourself to navigate through challenges with grace and composure. Embrace the power of finding calm amidst chaos and create a sense of inner peace that radiates to those around you.

Affirmations for savoring the little moments

1. "I fully immerse myself in the present moment, savoring the beauty it holds."

2. "I appreciate the small miracles and joys that exist in everyday life."

3. "I cultivate gratitude for the little moments that bring a smile to my face and warmth to my heart."

4. "I slow down and savor the sweetness of life's simple pleasures."

5. "I find joy in the smallest of details, allowing them to bring me immense happiness."

6. "I embrace the magic in the ordinary, finding wonder in the seemingly mundane."

7. "I take the time to pause and appreciate the blessings that surround me each day."

8. "I am fully present in each moment, cherishing it as a precious gift."

9. "I create space to savor the beauty of nature and the world around me."

10. "I find delight in the laughter and innocent playfulness of children."

11. "I treasure the moments of connection and love shared with family and friends."

12. "I take a moment to savor the taste, aroma, and texture of the food I eat, nourishing both my body and soul."

13. "I appreciate the warmth and coziness of my home, finding comfort and peace in its embrace."

14. "I notice the little acts of kindness and gestures of love that brighten my day."

15. "I cherish the quiet moments of solitude, allowing them to replenish my spirit."

16. "I embrace the joy in the journey, finding fulfillment in the process rather than solely focusing on the destination."

17. "I celebrate the small accomplishments and milestones, recognizing their significance in my growth."

18. "I am fully present with my loved ones, savoring the conversations, laughter, and shared experiences."

19. "I find delight in the sights, sounds, and scents of nature, appreciating its soothing and rejuvenating effects."

20. "I infuse each moment with mindfulness and gratitude, creating a tapestry of cherished memories."

Repeat these affirmations as a gentle reminder to slow down, be present, and savor the little moments that make life meaningful. By embracing a mindset of appreciation and gratitude, you invite more joy, wonder, and fulfillment into your everyday experiences. Take the time to savor the beauty and magic in the smallest details, and let these moments nourish your soul and bring you profound happiness.

Conclusion

Recap of the book's key concepts and affirmations

Throughout the book, "Affirmations Moms Actually Need," we have explored various key concepts and provided affirmations to support moms on their journey. Let's recap some of these key concepts and affirmations:

1. **Importance of affirmations for moms:**

   ○ Affirmations empower moms to cultivate self-belief, self-compassion, and resilience.

   ○ Affirmations provide a tool for nurturing well-being, releasing guilt, and embracing imperfections.

2. **Embracing self-care:**

   ○ Affirmations for setting boundaries and prioritizing self-care needs.

   ○ Affirmations for guilt-free self-care and prioritizing well-being.

3. **Overcoming mom guilt:**

   ○ Understanding the origins and effects of mom guilt.

   ○ Cultivating self-compassion and self-forgiveness.

○ Affirmations for releasing mom guilt, accepting imperfections, and acknowledging personal needs.

4. Building resilience:

○ Recognizing and managing stress and overwhelm.

○ Strengthening mental and emotional resilience.

○ Affirmations for coping with challenging moments, adapting to change, and finding balance amidst chaos.

5. Embracing imperfections:

○ Letting go of perfectionism and unrealistic expectations.

○ Celebrating the beauty of imperfections.

○ Affirmations for embracing self-acceptance, self-love, and body positivity.

6. Nurturing relationships:

○ Maintaining healthy relationships amidst motherhood.

○ Enhancing communication and connection.

○ Affirmations for strengthening romantic relationships, fostering friendships and support networks, and nurturing relationships with children.

7. Empowering mom's inner voice:

○ Harnessing the power of positive self-talk.

○ Affirmations for cultivating self-belief, recognizing personal achievements, and stepping into one's own power.

8. Practicing gratitude:

○ Understanding the transformative effects of gratitude.

○ Affirmations for cultivating a grateful mindset, appreciating the journey of motherhood, and finding joy in the present moment.

9. Embracing mindfulness:

- ○ Understanding the concept and benefits of mindfulness.

- ○ Cultivating mindfulness in everyday activities.

- ○ Affirmations for being present, mindful, grounding, and finding calm amidst chaos.

These key concepts and affirmations serve as valuable tools for moms to navigate the ups and downs of motherhood, embrace self-care, overcome guilt, build resilience, celebrate imperfections, nurture relationships, empower their inner voice, practice gratitude, and cultivate mindfulness.

As you embark on your personal journey as a mom, remember to embrace these concepts and affirmations as sources of inspiration, strength, and guidance. You are a remarkable and deserving mother, and by incorporating these affirmations into your daily life, you can create a positive and fulfilling experience for yourself and your loved ones.

Encouragement to integrate affirmations into daily life

Final thoughts on the journey of motherhood and self-growth

The journey of motherhood is a remarkable and transformative experience. It is a journey of unconditional love, selflessness, and growth. As you navigate the highs and lows of this journey, remember that it is also an opportunity for your own personal growth and self-discovery.

Motherhood challenges you to dig deep within yourself, to find strengths you never knew you had, and to embrace your imperfections with love and acceptance. It is a journey that requires resilience, adaptability, and a willingness to grow alongside your children.

Along the path of motherhood, remember these key points:

1. Embrace self-care: Prioritize your own well-being and self-care. Remember that taking care of yourself allows you to show up as the best version of yourself for your children and loved ones.

2. Let go of perfectionism: Embrace imperfections and let go of the need for everything to be perfect. It is in these imperfections that true beauty and growth can be found.

3. Practice self-compassion: Be gentle with yourself and practice self-compassion. Motherhood can be challenging, and it's okay to make mistakes or have tough

days. Treat yourself with the same love and kindness you give to your children.

4. Nurture your relationships: Cultivate meaningful connections with your loved ones, both within and outside your family. Surround yourself with a support network that uplifts you and provides a sense of belonging and understanding.

5. Embrace personal growth: Motherhood is an opportunity for personal growth and self-discovery. Allow yourself to evolve, learn from your experiences, and embrace the lessons that motherhood brings.

6. Practice gratitude: Cultivate a mindset of gratitude, finding joy and appreciation in the small moments and blessings that motherhood brings. Gratitude can shift your perspective and bring more fulfillment and joy to your journey.

7. Trust your intuition: You have a deep well of wisdom within you. Trust your instincts and intuition as you make decisions for yourself and your family. You know what is best for your children and yourself.

8. Celebrate the joys: Motherhood is filled with precious moments of joy, laughter, and love. Take the time to celebrate these moments and cherish the memories you create with your children.

Remember, you are not alone on this journey. Reach out for support when you need it, lean on your loved ones, and remember that there is no one "right" way to be a mother. Trust in yourself and your unique journey.

As you continue on your path of motherhood and self-growth, know that you are an incredible, loving, and capable mom. Embrace the lessons, celebrate the milestones, and cherish the journey. Your love and presence make a profound impact on the lives of your children, and the growth you experience along the way shapes you into an even more amazing version of yourself.

Wishing you an abundant and fulfilling journey as you navigate the beautiful and transformative role of motherhood. Embrace the growth, savor the moments, and always remember the incredible love that fills your heart as a mom.

www.ingramcontent.com/pod-product-compliance
Lightning Source LLC
Chambersburg PA
CBHW071307220526
45468CB00001B/292

* 9 7 8 1 9 6 9 5 6 3 7 2 0 *